The Art of Being Happy

The Art of Being Happy
A Philosophical Exploration

Evangeline Brooks

Mindful Pages

Published in 2023

ISBN: 9789358813043 (PB)
ISBN: 9789358815092 (eBook)

Published by

Mindful Pages
Imprint of Alpha Editions LLC
312 W. 2nd St #1834
Casper, WY 82601, USA

Contents

Introduction

In a world marked by complexity and rapid change, the pursuit of happiness remains a timeless and universal human aspiration. Yet, what does it truly mean to be happy? Is happiness a fleeting emotion, a long-term state of being, or something else entirely? These questions have fascinated philosophers, scholars, and thinkers for centuries. In this exploration of "The Philosophy of Happiness," we embark on a journey through the realms of philosophy, psychology, ethics, and culture to uncover the profound insights and diverse perspectives that shape our understanding of happiness.

As we navigate the intricate pathways of happiness, we will encounter ancient philosophical doctrines, modern psychological theories, and cultural wisdom from around the globe. We will delve into the nature of joy and contentment, examine the impact of personal values and societal factors, and ponder the ethical dilemmas that arise in the pursuit of happiness. Through this exploration, we aim to unravel the mysteries of human well-being and offer practical insights that can guide us toward a more fulfilling and meaningful existence.

In this book, we will embark on an intellectual journey through the complex and multifaceted world of happiness, exploring its philosophical underpinnings, psychological dimensions, cultural influences, and ethical considerations. Whether you are a philosopher, psychologist, or simply a curious seeker of a more fulfilling life, "The Philosophy of Happiness" invites you to join the conversation and contemplate the timeless pursuit of human well-being.

Join us on this intellectual and philosophical adventure as we unravel the multifaceted tapestry of happiness, seeking to answer age-old questions and perhaps discovering new perspectives along the way.

Chapter 1: Defining Happiness

Defining Happiness: A Multifaceted Journey into the Human Experience

Happiness, that elusive and cherished state of being, has captivated the human mind for millennia. It is a word that transcends cultures, languages, and ages, yet it remains one of the most challenging concepts to define precisely. Happiness is not a fixed destination, but rather a dynamic and multifaceted journey that varies from person to person and moment to moment. In our quest to understand and define happiness, we embark on an exploration of its many dimensions.

At its core, happiness is often associated with a deep sense of contentment, joy, and well-being. That warm, uplifting feeling permeates our being when we experience something delightful or achieve a long-sought goal. However, happiness is not a one-size-fits-all emotion. It manifests in various forms and degrees, ranging from the fleeting pleasure of savoring a piece of chocolate to the profound and enduring happiness of a life well-lived.

One traditional philosophical perspective on happiness comes from hedonism, which defines it as pursuing pleasure and avoiding pain. According to this view, happiness is synonymous with the maximization of pleasure and the minimization of suffering. While hedonism offers a straightforward definition, it oversimplifies the complexities of human emotions. Pleasure alone does not capture the richness of our experiences or the depth of our well-being.

A contrasting perspective, rooted in ancient Greek philosophy, is eudaimonia. Aristotle, one of the most influential philosophers in history, believed that true happiness, or eudaimonia, is achieved through flourishing one's innate human potential and cultivating virtue. It's not about the fleeting pleasures of the moment but rather the pursuit of a meaningful and purposeful life. This view recognizes that happiness is intimately connected to the development of our character, the pursuit of excellence, and the realization of our unique potential.

As we delve deeper into the quest to define happiness, we encounter cultural variations that shed light on its diverse manifestations. Different societies and cultures have their own concepts of happiness, influenced by their values, traditions, and beliefs. In some cultures, happiness may be linked to individual achievement and personal fulfillment, while in others, it may be deeply intertwined with community and social harmony. These cultural perspectives remind us that happiness is not only a personal experience but also a social and cultural construct.

In the realm of psychology, researchers have approached happiness from various angles. Positive psychology, a relatively new branch of psychology, focuses on the study of well-being and the factors that contribute to a fulfilling life. It explores the importance of positive emotions, engagement in meaningful activities, positive relationships, a sense of accomplishment, and a purpose in life as key components of happiness. This perspective highlights the dynamic nature of happiness and the role of personal growth and resilience in achieving it.

Defining happiness is further complicated by its ethical dimension. Can happiness be pursued at any cost, or are there ethical boundaries that should guide our pursuit? The pursuit of happiness can sometimes clash with moral principles, such as when personal gain comes at the expense of others. Ethical considerations remind us that the path to happiness is not a solitary one but is intricately woven into the fabric of our interactions with others.

In conclusion, defining happiness is a complex and multifaceted endeavor that encompasses a wide range of emotional, philosophical, cultural, psychological, and ethical dimensions. It is a journey that evolves as we navigate the intricacies of our lives, shape our values, and seek meaning and fulfillment. While there may never be a single, universally accepted definition of happiness, our exploration of its diverse facets enriches our understanding of the human experience and invites us to reflect on what it means to lead a truly happy life.

The Elusive Nature of Happiness

Happiness, often regarded as the ultimate pursuit of human life, is paradoxically one of the most elusive and enigmatic concepts known to humanity. Despite its universality, the nature of happiness is shrouded in complexity, subjectivity, and ever-shifting sands. This elusive quality of happiness is what makes it both a source of fascination and a formidable philosophical challenge.

At its heart, the elusive nature of happiness stems from its deeply subjective character. Happiness is not an external, quantifiable entity; rather, it resides within the intricate folds of individual consciousness. What brings joy and contentment to one person may not necessarily have the same effect on another. This subjectivity is rooted in the vast diversity of human experiences, backgrounds, and desires. It's a reminder that happiness is a deeply personal and ever-changing journey.

Furthermore, the pursuit of happiness often seems like chasing a fleeting butterfly. It can be here one moment and gone the next, leaving us pondering its ephemeral nature. Just when we think we have captured it, it slips through our fingers. This transitory quality of happiness is evident in the highs and lows of life. Moments of elation can be followed by periods of discontent, and the pursuit of continuous happiness can feel like an unending quest.

The philosopher Jean-Jacques Rousseau once stated, "Happiness: a good bank account, a good cook, and a good digestion." While his statement captures some aspects of happiness, it also highlights how it can be reduced to external factors that, while important, only scratch the surface. Happiness is not solely dependent on material wealth, culinary delights, or physical health. It goes beyond the tangible and touches the intangible realms of emotions, relationships, and meaning.

Moreover, the hedonic treadmill, a psychological concept, underscores the elusive nature of happiness. This theory suggests that humans have a baseline level of happiness to which they tend to return after both positive and negative events. Winning the lottery may provide a temporary surge in happiness, but individuals often revert to their baseline over time. Likewise, coping with adversity may initially reduce happiness, but individuals can adapt and return to their typical level of well-being. This phenomenon challenges the idea that constant external changes can lead to sustained happiness.

The elusive nature of happiness is further compounded by the influence of comparison and adaptation. People often gauge their happiness relative to others, leading to the "keeping up with the Joneses" mentality. This comparative aspect of happiness can create a perpetual cycle of discontent as individuals constantly strive for more, assuming that greater achievements or possessions will yield greater happiness. However, this pursuit can be a mirage, as adaptation tends to level the playing field over time.

Despite these challenges, the elusive nature of happiness is not a cause for despair. Instead, it invites us to explore the depths of our own inner world and to cultivate a more nuanced understanding of what truly brings us joy and fulfillment. It prompts us to recognize that happiness is not a fixed destination but a continuous journey influenced by our thoughts, actions, and perceptions.

In conclusion, the elusive nature of happiness is a paradox that has intrigued philosophers, psychologists, and individuals from all walks of life throughout history. It is a reminder that happiness is not a one-size-fits-all concept but a deeply personal and ever-evolving experience. Embracing this complexity can lead to a more authentic and profound exploration of what it means to live a happy and meaningful life. Rather than chasing a fleeting illusion, we may discover that happiness is a treasure hidden within ourselves, waiting to be unearthed through self-awareness, purpose, and the appreciation of life's small but beautiful moments

Philosophical Explorations of Happiness: Insights from the Great Thinkers

Happiness, often described as the ultimate human pursuit, has been a central theme in philosophy for centuries. Philosophers from diverse traditions and eras have engaged in profound explorations of happiness, delving into its nature, sources, and implications for the human experience. These philosophical investigations offer us invaluable insights into the essence of a fulfilling life.

Eudaimonia: Aristotle's Pursuit of the Good Life

Aristotle, one of the most influential figures in Western philosophy, proposed a concept of happiness known as eudaimonia. In Aristotle's view, happiness was not merely the pursuit of pleasure, as hedonists argued, but the realization of one's true potential and the cultivation of virtues. He believed that a virtuous and contemplative life led to eudaimonia, a state of flourishing. According to Aristotle, the good life is one in which individuals strive for moral excellence, engage in meaningful activities, and attain a sense of purpose. His perspective on happiness transcends the fleeting pleasures of the moment, emphasizing the importance of a well-lived life deeply rooted in ethics and self-fulfillment.

Utilitarianism: Maximizing Pleasure and Minimizing Pain

The utilitarian philosophy, championed by figures like Jeremy Bentham and John Stuart Mill, takes a different approach to happiness. It posits that happiness is the highest good and that actions should be judged based on their ability to maximize overall happiness while minimizing suffering. This utilitarian calculus seeks to quantify happiness and assign values to different experiences. While it offers a clear framework for ethical decision-making, it has also been criticized for reducing happiness to a mere mathematical equation and failing to account for individual rights and justice.

Hedonism: The Pursuit of Pleasure

Hedonistic philosophies, in contrast to Aristotle's eudaimonia, posit that happiness is synonymous with pursuing pleasure and avoiding pain. Ancient hedonists like Epicurus believed that the highest form of happiness came from the absence of physical and mental distress, which they termed "ataraxia." Contemporary hedonism often associates happiness with the relentless pursuit of immediate pleasures, sometimes at the expense of long-term well-being. While hedonism can offer moments of delight, it often falls short in providing lasting and meaningful happiness, as it may neglect the pursuit of deeper, more enduring forms of well-being.

Existentialism: Navigating the Absurd for Authentic Happiness

Existentialist philosophers such as Jean-Paul Sartre and Albert Camus grappled with the human condition in a world devoid of inherent meaning. They argued that individuals must confront the inherent absurdity of life and create their own meaning and values. In this existentialist pursuit, happiness is not found in the avoidance of life's challenges but in the authentic engagement with them. Existentialism acknowledges the complexities and sometimes inherent suffering of human existence but encourages individuals to find purpose and happiness through their choices and actions.

Virtue Ethics: Balancing Character and Action

Virtue ethics, as expounded by philosophers like Plato and Confucius, emphasizes the development of virtuous character as the foundation of a fulfilling life. Happiness, in this context, is closely tied to moral excellence and ethical living. Virtue ethicists argue that cultivating virtues such as courage, compassion, and wisdom leads to a more meaningful and flourishing existence. This philosophical approach recognizes the intrinsic connection between one's character and the ethical quality of their actions, suggesting that happiness is intimately intertwined with the pursuit of virtue.

In conclusion, philosophical explorations of happiness offer diverse perspectives on the nature and pursuit of well-being. From Aristotle's eudaimonia to the utilitarian pursuit of pleasure, these philosophies provide frameworks for understanding what it means to lead a fulfilling life. They challenge us to reflect on the sources of our happiness, the role of ethics, and the nature of the human experience. While these philosophical traditions may differ in their approaches, they all contribute to a broader conversation about the essence of happiness and the paths we can take to achieve it. Ultimately, the quest for happiness is a profound and enduring inquiry that continues to inspire philosophical reflection and personal exploration.

Psychological Dimensions of Well-being: Navigating the Complex Landscape of Human Happiness

Well-being, a term synonymous with happiness and life satisfaction, is a multifaceted concept that encompasses a wide array of psychological dimensions. It goes beyond mere absence of distress and taps into the deeper aspects of human experience, exploring the positive emotions, personal strengths, and meaningful connections that contribute to a fulfilled life. In this exploration of the psychological dimensions of well-being, we delve into the complexities of human happiness and the factors that shape our sense of well-being.

Positive Emotions: The Building Blocks of Well-being

Positive psychology, a branch of psychology dedicated to the study of well-being and human flourishing, places a significant emphasis on positive emotions as key components of well-being. Positive emotions such as joy, gratitude, love, and awe are pleasant experiences in themselves and contribute to overall well-being. These emotions can enhance our resilience in the face of adversity, broaden our perspectives, and foster positive social interactions. They act as the building blocks upon which a sense of well-being is constructed.

Positive psychologists like Martin Seligman have argued that cultivating a repertoire of positive emotions is crucial for increasing well-being. By savoring life's small pleasures, practicing gratitude, and nurturing positive relationships, individuals can enhance their overall psychological well-being.

Engagement and Flow: The Joy of Immersion

Well-being isn't just about experiencing positive emotions; it also involves engaging in activities that absorb our attention and provide a sense of purpose. This state of absorption and focused attention is often referred to as "flow," a concept introduced by psychologist CC. When we are in a state of flow, we lose track of time, experience deep concentration, and derive a sense of satisfaction from the activity.

Engagement in such activities contributes to our psychological well-being by providing a sense of mastery and accomplishment. Whether it's a creative pursuit, a challenging work task, or a fulfilling hobby, these engagements offer a profound sense of purpose and contribute to our overall happiness.

Meaning and Purpose: A Fulfilling Life Narrative

Well-being extends beyond momentary experiences and encompasses a broader sense of meaning and purpose in life. Psychologist Viktor Frankl, a Holocaust survivor, emphasized the significance of finding meaning even in dire circumstances. He argued that individuals who can identify a sense of purpose and meaning in their lives are more resilient and have a higher sense of well-being.

Finding meaning often involves understanding one's values, beliefs, and personal narratives. It's about creating a life story that aligns with one's core values and aspirations. This dimension of well-being emphasizes the importance of self-reflection, self-discovery, and the pursuit of goals that transcend immediate gratification.

Positive Relationships: The Social Fabric of Well-being

Human beings are inherently social creatures, and our well-being is deeply intertwined with the quality of our relationships. Positive psychology highlights the significance of positive social interactions and connections as crucial contributors to well-being.

Maintaining close relationships, experiencing social support, and engaging in acts of kindness and empathy are all aspects of positive relationships that enhance well-being. Positive interactions with others not only boost our emotional state but also provide a buffer against stress and adversity.

Resilience and Coping: Navigating Life's Challenges

Well-being is not a static state but a dynamic process that involves coping with life's challenges and setbacks. Psychological resilience, the ability to bounce back from adversity, is a critical dimension of well-being. Resilient individuals are better equipped to adapt to difficult circumstances, maintain a positive outlook, and continue to pursue their goals despite obstacles.

Resilience is not a fixed trait but a skill that can be cultivated through various strategies, including cognitive reframing, seeking social support, and developing problem-solving skills. These psychological dimensions contribute to an individual's ability to maintain well-being in the face of life's ups and downs.

In conclusion, the psychological dimensions of well-being encompass a rich tapestry of positive emotions, engagement, meaning, positive relationships, and resilience. Together, they form the complex landscape of human happiness and provide a framework for understanding the multifaceted nature of well-being. Nurturing these dimensions in our lives involves self-awareness, intentional choices, and the recognition that well-being is an ongoing journey of self-discovery and growth. By cultivating these psychological dimensions, individuals can enhance their overall sense of well-being and lead more fulfilling and meaningful lives.

Chapter 2: The Pursuit of Pleasure: Hedonism

Hedonism, as a philosophical doctrine, centers on the notion that pleasure is the ultimate and intrinsic good, and the pursuit of pleasure is the primary aim of human existence. It's a concept that has intrigued and provoked thought for centuries, with its roots reaching back to ancient Greece. In this exploration of hedonism, we will delve into its essence, confront the paradox it presents, and examine some of the primary critiques it has faced.

Hedonism: The Philosophy of Pleasure

At its core, hedonism posits that pleasure is the highest good and pain is the greatest evil. This foundational belief leads to the view that life's ethical and moral goal is the maximization of pleasure and the minimization of pain. Hedonistic philosophies often differ in their approach to pleasure, distinguishing between various types and sources of pleasure.

Psychological Hedonism vs. Ethical Hedonism: Psychological hedonism asserts that all human actions are ultimately driven by the pursuit of pleasure or the avoidance of pain. It posits that pleasure is the underlying motivator for every choice, whether consciously or subconsciously. Ethical hedonism, on the other hand, goes beyond this psychological aspect and asserts that one should actively seek pleasure and avoid pain as a matter of ethical duty.

Quantitative vs. Qualitative Hedonism: Within the realm of hedonism, there's also a distinction between those who focus on the quantity of pleasure and those who emphasize its quality. Quantitative hedonists argue that the goal is to maximize the net balance of pleasure over pain, regardless of the sources of pleasure. Qualitative hedonists, on the other hand, argue that some forms of pleasure are superior to others, valuing intellectual, artistic, or spiritual joys more highly than base physical ones.

The Pleasure-Pain Paradox

While hedonism extols the virtues of pleasure, it's not without its paradoxes and challenges. One of the most significant paradoxes is the "pleasure-pain paradox," which raises questions about whether the relentless pursuit of pleasure is a sustainable path to happiness.

The Paradox Itself: The paradox arises from the observation that the unrestrained pursuit of immediate pleasures can often lead to negative consequences and pain in the long run. For instance, indulgence in excessive food or drink may provide short-term pleasure but can result in health problems or regret afterward. Similarly, seeking instant gratification through impulsive actions can lead to pain and suffering over time.

Diminishing Returns: Another aspect of the paradox is the concept of diminishing returns, where the pleasure derived from a particular source decrease with repeated exposure. This means that what once brought immense pleasure may eventually become less satisfying, prompting individuals to seek more extreme or novel experiences in the quest for happiness.

Critiques of Hedonism

Hedonism has not escaped criticism, and various critiques have been leveled against it throughout history.

Lack of Consideration for Other Values: One of the primary critiques of hedonism is its exclusive focus on pleasure, often neglecting other moral values such as justice, fairness, and autonomy. Critics argue that some actions, even if they provide pleasure, can be morally wrong or ethically questionable. For instance, stealing might bring pleasure to the thief but is deemed immoral because it violates principles of fairness and property rights.

Short-Term vs. Long-Term Well-being: Critics also contend that hedonism often prioritizes short-term pleasures at the expense of long-term well-being. The pursuit of immediate gratification can lead to impulsive decision-making and a neglect of future consequences, potentially resulting in negative outcomes and reduced overall well-being.

Complexity of Pleasure: Defining what constitutes pleasure can be a contentious issue within hedonism. Different individuals may experience and value pleasure differently, making it challenging to create a universal framework for evaluating happiness. Additionally, some pleasures may be derived from complex intellectual or emotional experiences that are difficult to quantify or compare.

In conclusion, hedonism, with its focus on pleasure as the ultimate good, offers a straightforward approach to understanding well-being. However, it is not without its paradoxes and critiques. Whether viewed through the lens of psychological or ethical hedonism, or considering the nuances of pleasure and pain, the pursuit of pleasure remains a topic of philosophical contemplation, challenging us to grapple with fundamental questions about the nature of happiness and the ethical implications of our desires

Chapter 3: Eudaimonia: Flourishing and Virtue

Eudaimonia: Flourishing and Virtue

Eudaimonia, a concept originating from ancient Greek philosophy, represents the pursuit of flourishing and the highest state of human well-being. It is a complex and multifaceted idea that has been explored and refined over the centuries. In this exploration of eudaimonia, we will delve into its historical roots, the virtue ethics associated with it, and its modern interpretations.

Aristotle and the Quest for Eudaimonia

Aristotle, one of the most influential philosophers in history, played a pivotal role in shaping the concept of eudaimonia. For Aristotle, eudaimonia was not a fleeting emotion or the pursuit of physical pleasure but a state of flourishing that could be achieved through cultivating virtue and realising one's true potential.

Virtue as the Foundation: Aristotle argued that virtue was the cornerstone of eudaimonia. Virtues, such as courage, wisdom, justice, and temperance, were moral and character traits that enabled individuals to live a life of excellence. Virtuous actions were seen as how one could achieve eudaimonia.

The Doctrine of the Mean: Aristotle introduced the "doctrine of the mean" to guide virtuous behavior. According to this doctrine, virtues are the golden mean between extremes. For example, courage is the virtue between recklessness and cowardice. Finding the right balance in one's actions and emotions was considered crucial for eudaimonia.

Contemplation and Intellectual Virtue: Aristotle also emphasized the importance of intellectual virtues, particularly the virtue of contemplation or philosophical wisdom. He believed that the pursuit of knowledge and the contemplation of abstract truths were among the highest human activities, contributing significantly to eudaimonia.

Virtue Ethics and the Good Life

Eudaimonia is intimately connected with virtue ethics, a moral philosophy that emphasizes the development of virtuous character as the foundation of ethical living. Virtue ethicists, following Aristotle's lead, argue that the good life is one in which individuals strive for moral excellence, engage in meaningful activities, and attain a sense of purpose.

The Role of Virtue: Virtue ethics places a strong emphasis on personal virtues as the keys to leading a good life. Virtues such as honesty, compassion, integrity, and kindness are considered morally commendable and essential for eudaimonia.

Ethical Decision-Making: Virtue ethics provides a framework for ethical decision-making that focuses on the character of the individual rather than following a set of rigid rules or consequences-based calculations. It encourages individuals to act in alignment with their virtues and values.

Virtue as a Lifelong Journey: Virtue ethicists recognize that becoming virtuous is lifelong. It involves self-reflection, self-improvement, and the pursuit of moral growth. The aim is not just to do good deeds but to become a good person.

Modern Interpretations of Eudaimonia

In contemporary philosophy, eudaimonia has found renewed interest and relevance. Modern interpretations of eudaimonia build upon Aristotle's ideas but adapt them to the complexities of the modern world.

Subjective Well-being: Some modern interpretations of eudaimonia incorporate aspects of subjective well-being, acknowledging that individual happiness and life satisfaction play a role in flourishing. However, they still emphasize the importance of virtue and personal growth.

Human Flourishing in a Complex World: Modern interpretations of eudaimonia recognize that flourishing is not a one-size-fits-all concept. It takes into account the individual's unique strengths, values, and circumstances, acknowledging that the path to flourishing may vary from person to person.

Balancing Personal Fulfillment and Contribution to Society: Many contemporary interpretations of eudaimonia emphasize the importance of balancing personal fulfillment with contributing to the greater good of society. Flourishing is seen as not only a state of personal well-being but also a way of positively impacting the world.

In conclusion, eudaimonia, as a pursuit of flourishing and virtue, has deep historical roots in the philosophy of Aristotle and virtue ethics. It continues to evolve and adapt in contemporary thought, offering a compelling perspective on the nature of a good and fulfilling life. Whether viewed through the lens of classical virtue ethics or modern interpretations that consider subjective well-being and the complexities of the modern world, eudaimonia invites us to reflect on what it means to live a life of excellence and purpose.

Chapter 4: The Role of Culture

Culture, as a multifaceted and dynamic concept, plays a pivotal role in shaping various aspects of human life, including happiness. This chapter explores the influence of culture on well-being, with a specific focus on the variations in happiness across different cultures.

Cultural Variations in Happiness

Happiness, despite its universality as an emotional experience, is subject to significant variations across cultures. These variations are rooted in cultural norms, values, beliefs, and social structures. Here, we delve into the fascinating realm of cultural variations in happiness.

Cultural Definitions of Happiness: Different cultures may have distinct definitions and conceptualizations of happiness. For instance, Western cultures often emphasize individual achievement, personal fulfillment, and the pursuit of happiness as a fundamental right. In contrast, some Eastern cultures may prioritize collective well-being, social harmony, and the suppression of individual desires for the greater good.

Collectivism vs. Individualism: Cultural variations in happiness are often linked to the degree of collectivism or individualism within a society. Collectivist cultures, prevalent in many Asian countries, strongly emphasise group harmony and interconnectedness. Happiness in collectivist cultures may be closely tied to family relationships, community involvement, and conformity to social norms. In contrast, individualist cultures, common in Western societies, prioritize personal autonomy and self-expression, leading to different factors contributing to happiness.

Cultural Norms and Expectations: Cultural norms and expectations shape individuals' aspirations and sources of happiness. In some cultures, success might be defined by achieving high academic or professional status, while in others, it could be associated with fulfilling family and community roles. Cultural expectations can create unique pressures and influences on individual well-being.

Cultural Practices and Rituals: Cultural practices and rituals often have a profound impact on happiness. Festivals, ceremonies, and traditions can contribute to a sense of belonging, identity, and joy. For example, the celebration of Chinese New Year or Diwali in India involves family gatherings, feasting, and cultural rituals that foster happiness and a sense of community.

Impact of Socioeconomic Factors: Economic and socioeconomic conditions within a culture can significantly affect happiness levels. Cultures with greater economic stability and access to resources may experience higher levels of happiness due to improved living standards, access to education, and healthcare. Conversely, cultures facing economic hardship and inequality may struggle to maintain high levels of well-being.

Cultural Values and Well-being: Cultural values, such as the importance of work, leisure, family, spirituality, and materialism, can shape the pursuit of happiness. For example, cultures prioritising material success may emphasise financial achievement as a source of happiness, while cultures valuing spirituality may find fulfillment through religious practices and transcendental experiences.

Cross-Cultural Research on Happiness: Cross-cultural research on happiness involves comparing well-being across different cultures. This research has revealed fascinating insights, such as the finding that certain cultures report higher levels of life satisfaction despite lower income levels, suggesting that cultural factors play a significant role in shaping happiness.

Challenges and Adaptations: As cultures evolve and encounter globalization and changing social dynamics, individuals may face challenges in reconciling traditional cultural values with modern aspirations. Some cultures adapt by integrating new elements into their well-being frameworks, while others may struggle to maintain cultural integrity in the face of external influences.

Culture exerts a profound influence on the understanding and pursuit of happiness. Recognizing the cultural variations in happiness allows us to appreciate the diversity of human experiences and offers valuable insights for promoting well-being in culturally sensitive ways. Whether by studying the impact of cultural norms, understanding the interplay between individualism and collectivism, or exploring the role of cultural practices and values, the study of culture and happiness enriches our understanding of the human condition

The Influence of Cultural Values

The influence of cultural values on individuals and societies is profound, shaping beliefs, behaviors, and worldviews. These values, often deeply ingrained and passed down through generations, serve as guiding principles that dictate how individuals interact with each other and their environment. Understanding the impact of cultural values is essential for appreciating the rich tapestry of human diversity and for navigating the complexities of an increasingly interconnected world.

1. Shaping Identity and Belief Systems: Cultural values play a pivotal role in shaping individual and collective identities. They inform a person's sense of self, providing a framework for understanding their role within the cultural group. These values also influence belief systems, including religious, moral, and ethical perspectives. For example, a culture that values community and collectivism may prioritize communal well-being and social harmony, whereas a culture that values individualism may emphasize personal autonomy and achievement.

2. Guiding Behavior and Social Norms: Cultural values serve as the foundation for social norms and acceptable behaviors within a given society. They define what is considered right or wrong, appropriate or inappropriate. These norms, in turn, regulate interactions, relationships, and social expectations. For instance, a culture that values respect for authority figures may have strict hierarchies and deferential behavior, while a culture that values egalitarianism may promote more equitable social dynamics.

3. Influencing Decision-Making: Cultural values influence decision-making processes, including choices related to education, career, relationships, and lifestyle. These values provide a moral compass that guides individuals in making choices aligned with their cultural identity. For instance, a culture that values familial loyalty may prioritize caregiving responsibilities, even if it requires sacrificing personal ambitions.

4. Shaping Communication and Language: Cultural values are embedded in language and communication styles. They determine how individuals express themselves, convey emotions, and engage in verbal and nonverbal communication. Understanding these cultural nuances is vital for effective cross-cultural interactions and avoiding misunderstandings.

5. Impact on Social Institutions and Policies: Cultural values influence the development of social institutions and policies within a society. Laws, governance structures, and societal norms often reflect the prevailing cultural values. For example, cultures that prioritize individual freedoms may have policies emphasizing personal liberties, while cultures valuing communal well-being may prioritize social welfare programs.

In essence, the influence of cultural values permeates every facet of human existence, from personal identity to societal structures. Recognizing and respecting these values is essential for promoting cultural sensitivity, fostering intercultural understanding, and building harmonious relationships in an increasingly diverse global community

Happiness in a Globalized World

In our contemporary globalized world, the pursuit of happiness has taken on new dimensions and challenges. As societies become more interconnected and individuals are exposed to diverse cultures, values, and lifestyles, the quest for well-being has evolved in both its opportunities and complexities. This exploration delves into the various facets of happiness in a globalized world, addressing the cultural influences, technological advancements, and societal shifts that shape our understanding of well-being.

Cultural Diversity and Well-being

One of the defining features of globalization is the intermingling of cultures from around the world. As individuals encounter diverse belief systems, traditions, and lifestyles, their notions of happiness become enriched and expanded. Exposure to different cultural perspectives can lead to a more inclusive understanding of well-being, acknowledging that there are various paths to happiness.

However, cultural diversity can also present challenges. Cultural clashes and misunderstandings may arise, impacting an individual's sense of belonging and well-being. Navigating this diversity requires cultural sensitivity, empathy, and a willingness to embrace the richness of global cultural tapestry while honoring one's own cultural roots.

Technological Advancements and Their Impact

The digital age, driven by technological innovations, has transformed the way we perceive and pursue happiness. The internet, social media, and digital platforms have created unprecedented opportunities for connection, information-sharing, and self-expression. These advancements have opened new avenues for global communication, enabling people to form relationships and communities that transcend geographical boundaries.

However, the pervasive presence of technology also poses challenges to well-being. The constant barrage of information, social comparison, and the addictive nature of digital platforms can lead to anxiety, depression, and a sense of disconnection. Striking a balance between the benefits and drawbacks of technology is crucial for maintaining happiness in a globalized world.

Economic Interdependence and Materialism

Globalization has led to increased economic interdependence among nations, resulting in heightened competition and consumerism. The pursuit of material wealth and success is often prioritized in a globalized society, with the belief that material possessions and financial achievements are synonymous with happiness.

However, the relentless pursuit of materialism can have adverse effects on well-being. The pressure to attain material success can lead to stress, overwork, and a neglect of personal relationships and inner fulfillment. In a globalized world, it is essential to question whether the accumulation of material wealth truly equates to lasting happiness or if there are alternative measures of well-being that deserve more attention.

Social and Environmental Concerns

Globalization has brought attention to pressing social and environmental issues that have a direct impact on well-being. Concerns such as climate change, inequality, and social justice have become global conversations, influencing individuals' perceptions of happiness. Many people find purpose and well-being in advocating for positive change and working towards a more equitable and sustainable world.

At the same time, these global challenges can evoke feelings of anxiety, powerlessness, and despair. Navigating the tension between awareness of these issues and maintaining personal well-being is a significant challenge in a globalized world. Finding a sense of agency and optimism amidst global crises is a testament to human resilience and the capacity for happiness even in the face of adversity.

Happiness in a globalized world is a multifaceted and dynamic concept. It is influenced by cultural diversity, technological advancements, economic interdependence, social and environmental concerns, and individual choices. Navigating the complexities of well-being in this context requires a nuanced understanding of the interconnectedness of our world and the recognition that happiness is not a fixed destination but an ongoing journey.

Ultimately, happiness in a globalized world is about finding meaning, connection, and fulfillment in a rapidly changing and interconnected global society. It is a reminder that our pursuit of well-being is not isolated from the broader human experience but is deeply intertwined with the collective journey of humanity towards a more inclusive, compassionate, and sustainable world.

Chapter 5: The Pursuit of Meaning: Existentialism and Beyond

In the realm of philosophy and the quest for a meaningful existence, existentialism stands as a potent and often provocative approach. Emerging in the late 19th and early 20th centuries, existentialism challenges traditional notions of happiness and well-being. It invites individuals to grapple with profound questions about the human condition, freedom, choice, and the ultimate search for meaning in a seemingly indifferent world. This exploration delves into existentialism and its departure from conventional paradigms of happiness, offering insights into the pursuit of telling beyond pleasure and virtue.

Beyond Pleasure and Virtue: Existentialist Perspectives

As a philosophical movement, existentialism diverges from traditional views of happiness rooted in pleasure or virtue. It propounds the idea that the pursuit of meaning is a fundamental aspect of human existence and can transcend the quest for fun and cultivating virtues.

Existentialism introduces several key concepts that reshape our understanding of happiness:

1. The Absurdity of Existence

Existentialist thinkers like Albert Camus and Jean-Paul Sartre confront the absurdity of human existence. They argue that life lacks inherent meaning, and the universe is indifferent to human concerns. In this context, pursuing pleasure or adherence to moral virtues can be seen as arbitrary and futile. Existentialists invite individuals to acknowledge the absurdity of life and make choices in the face of this inherent meaninglessness.

2. Authenticity and Freedom

Existentialism places a strong emphasis on individual freedom and authenticity. Existentialist philosophers contend that true happiness arises when individuals confront their freedom to make choices and accept the responsibilities that come with it. Realism, in this context, means living in accordance with one's values, beliefs, and personal truths, even in the face of existential uncertainty.

3. The Search for Meaning

Existentialists argue that the pursuit of meaning is a fundamental human drive. While pleasure and virtue can be components of a meaningful life, existentialism suggests that the search for meaning often transcends these conventional notions. Meaning may emerge from personal passions, creative pursuits, genuine relationships, or acts of self-transcendence.

4. Embracing the Full Range of Human Experience

Existentialism encourages individuals to embrace the full spectrum of human experience, including moments of despair, suffering, and doubt. Rather than seeking to avoid or numb these experiences, existentialists argue that they are integral to the human condition and can lead to profound insights and growth.

5. The Role of Responsibility

Existentialism emphasizes the role of personal responsibility in creating a meaningful life. Existentialist philosophers assert that individuals are responsible for defining their own values and creating their own meaning. This burden of responsibility can be daunting, but it is also liberating, as it grants individuals the agency to shape their own lives.

Examples from Existentialist Literature

Existentialist literature often serves as a poignant illustration of these concepts. In Albert Camus' novel "The Stranger," the protagonist, Meursault, grapples with the absurdity of life and the indifference of the universe. His journey is an existential exploration of authenticity, freedom, and the pursuit of meaning beyond conventional notions of happiness.

Similarly, Jean-Paul Sartre's play "No Exit" delves into the complexities of human relationships and individuals' choices in the face of existential uncertainty. The characters in the play are confined to a room, forced to confront their own actions and the consequences of their choices. It serves as a powerful examination of authenticity and personal responsibility.

Beyond Pleasure and Virtue: Contemporary Relevance

While existentialism emerged in the 20th century, its perspectives continue to resonate in contemporary thought. In a world marked by rapid change, uncertainty, and the search for deeper meaning, existentialist ideas offer valuable insights for individuals navigating the complexities of modern life.

1. Embracing Complexity

Existentialism encourages individuals to embrace the complexity of their own existence. In a globalized world with diverse cultures, belief systems, and value frameworks, existentialism's call to confront the complexities of life is particularly relevant. It invites individuals to engage with diverse perspectives and navigate the nuanced terrain of cross-cultural interactions.

2. The Challenge of Authenticity

In an era of social media and digital personas, the concept of authenticity takes on heightened importance. Existentialism reminds us that true happiness arises when we are authentic to ourselves, rather than conforming to societal expectations or performing for others. This message is especially pertinent in a world where external validation and image projection often dominate social dynamics.

3. The Search for Meaning in a Rapidly Changing World

The pursuit of meaning remains a central human concern in contemporary society. As individuals grapple with the challenges of technological advancements, climate change, and social transformations, existentialism's emphasis on personal responsibility and the search for meaning offers a compass for navigating these turbulent times.

Existentialism challenges us to reevaluate traditional notions of happiness rooted in pleasure and virtue. Instead, it invites us to embrace the complexities of the human experience, confront the absurdity of existence, and search for meaning in a world that often defies easy answers. While existentialism may not provide a definitive roadmap to happiness, it offers a profound perspective on the enduring human quest for a life of depth, authenticity, and significance. In a globalized world where cultural, social, and technological shifts continue to reshape the human experience, existentialism's insights remain as relevant as ever.

The Search for Meaning and Purpose

The search for meaning and purpose is an intrinsic and enduring aspect of the human experience. It represents a profound journey of self-discovery, personal growth, and the quest for fulfillment that transcends cultural, societal, and individual boundaries. This exploration delves into the significance of the search for meaning and purpose, the factors that contribute to it, and its impact on our lives.

The Significance of Meaning and Purpose

At its core, the search for meaning and purpose is about seeking a deeper understanding of one's existence and the world around them. It encompasses questions such as: What is the purpose of life? Why am I here? What gives my life meaning? These existential inquiries are fundamental to human consciousness and reflect our innate desire to make sense of our experiences.

Motivation for the Search

Several factors motivate individuals to embark on the search for meaning and purpose:

Existential Awareness: As individuals become aware of their mortality and the finite nature of life, they are often prompted to contemplate the more profound significance of their existence. This awareness can catalyze seeking meaning and purpose.

Transitions and Milestones: Life transitions, such as graduating from school, starting a family, or facing significant losses, often prompt individuals to reevaluate their goals, values, and priorities, leading to a search for deeper meaning.

Intrinsic Curiosity: Inherent human curiosity drives individuals to explore the mysteries of existence, ponder philosophical questions, and engage in introspective reflection.

Psychological Well-being: Research in psychology suggests that a sense of purpose and meaning is associated with greater psychological well-being, including increased life satisfaction, resilience, and reduced symptoms of anxiety and depression. This knowledge motivates many to actively seek these elements in their lives.

Dimensions of Meaning and Purpose

The quest for meaning and purpose can manifest in various dimensions:

Personal Fulfillment: Individuals often seek meaning through personal accomplishments, creative pursuits, and the realization of their potential. This dimension focuses on achieving individual goals and aspirations.

Social Connection: Many find meaning and purpose in their relationships, emphasizing the importance of connection, empathy, and contributing to the well-being of loved ones and communities.

Spirituality and Transcendence: For some, meaning and purpose are deeply intertwined with spiritual or metaphysical experiences. This dimension involves seeking a higher purpose or connection with a divine or cosmic reality.

Contributing to the Greater Good: A sense of purpose can also be derived from contributing to a cause larger than oneself. Individuals find meaning in positively impacting society through volunteering, activism, or philanthropy.

Challenges in the Search

The search for meaning and purpose is not without its challenges:

Existential Anxiety: Contemplating life's fundamental questions can evoke existential anxiety and distress. Facing the uncertainty of existence and the potential absence of inherent meaning can be deeply unsettling.

External Pressures: Societal expectations and external pressures can sometimes lead individuals to pursue paths that are incongruent with their true values and aspirations, diverting them from their authentic search for meaning.

Changing Priorities: As life circumstances evolve, individuals may need to adapt their pursuit of meaning and purpose. Balancing personal, professional, and societal demands can be a complex task.

Cultural Variations: Cultural backgrounds and belief systems shape individuals' perspectives on meaning and purpose. What is meaningful for one person may differ significantly from another based on cultural influences.

Impact on Well-being

Research consistently demonstrates that a sense of meaning and purpose positively impacts well-being. It is associated with increased life satisfaction, greater resilience in the face of adversity, reduced symptoms of psychological distress, and improved overall mental health. Additionally, individuals who perceive their lives as meaningful are often more motivated, creative, and productive.

The search for meaning and purpose is an enduring and deeply human quest. It reflects our intrinsic desire to find significance in our lives, make sense of the world, and cultivate a sense of fulfillment. While this journey can be challenging and fraught with existential questions, it is also profoundly rewarding. Ultimately, pursuing meaning and purpose enriches our lives, imbuing them with depth, authenticity, and a sense of connectedness to something greater than ourselves. Whether through personal fulfillment, social connection, spirituality, or contributing to the greater good, the search for meaning and purpose remains a fundamental and transformative aspect of the human experience.

Balancing Hedonism, Eudaimonia, and Existentialism: A Complex Pursuit of Well-being

The quest for well-being and fulfilvarious philosophical perspectives, including hedonism, eudaimonia, and existentialism can informlment is a multifaceted journey that can be informed by various philosophical perspectives, including hedonism, eudaimonia, and existentialism. Each of these philosophies offers a distinct approach to understanding and achieving well-being, and individuals often grapple with how to balance these perspectives in their lives.

Hedonism: The Pursuit of Pleasure and Enjoyment

Hedonism, as a philosophical doctrine, places pleasure at the forefront of well-being. It contends that the pursuit of pleasure and the avoidance of pain are the primary drivers of human actions. While hedonism has been criticized for its simplicity and potential for short-sightedness, it underscores the importance of experiencing joy and contentment in life.

Eudaimonia: Flourishing and Virtue

Eudaimonia, rooted in the teachings of philosophers like Aristotle, centers on flourishing and cultivating virtues as essential components of well-being. It emphasizes the importance of living a life of excellence, guided by moral and ethical virtues, and fulfilling one's potential. Eudaimonia encourages individuals to seek deeper, long-lasting sources of well-being beyond momentary pleasures.

Existentialism: Confronting Life's Absurdity

In contrast, existentialism grapples with life's inherent meaninglessness and absurdity. Existentialist thinkers like Jean-Paul Sartre and Albert Camus argue that life lacks intrinsic purpose, and individuals must confront the void and make choices in the face of existential uncertainty. Existentialism invites individuals to embrace their freedom, authenticity, and responsibility.

Balancing Perspectives for Well-being

Achieving a balanced approach to well-being that incorporates elements of hedonism, eudaimonia, and existentialism requires a nuanced understanding of the strengths and limitations of each philosophy. Here are some ways in which individuals can balance these perspectives:

1. Recognize the Value of Pleasure: Hedonism reminds us of the importance of experiencing pleasure and enjoyment in life. Embracing moments of joy, relaxation, and indulgence can enhance our overall well-being. However, avoiding excessive or self-destructive hedonism is essential, which may lead to short-term gratification at the expense of long-term fulfillment.

2. Cultivate Virtues: Eudaimonia underscores the significance of moral and ethical virtues in living a meaningful life. Practicing virtues like compassion, integrity, and wisdom can contribute to a sense of purpose and fulfillment. Integrating these virtues into daily choices and actions fosters a deeper form of well-being that transcends momentary pleasures.

3. Embrace Freedom and Responsibility: Existentialism encourages individuals to confront the existential void and make choices that align with their authentic values. Recognizing the freedom to shape our lives and accepting responsibility for our choices empowers us to create a sense of purpose and meaning. Existentialism reminds us that, without inherent meaning, we can define our paths.

4. Seek Balance and Integration: Balancing these philosophical perspectives is not about choosing one over the others but integrating them into a coherent framework for well-being. This may involve identifying areas where hedonistic pleasures align with virtuous living or where existential choices lead to deeper enjoyment.

5. Reflect and Evolve: Finding a balanced approach to well-being is an ongoing process that requires reflection and adaptation. Life circumstances change, and individual values and priorities may evolve. Regular self-examination can help individuals adjust their approach to align with their current understanding of well-being.

Balancing hedonism, eudaimonia, and existentialism in the pursuit of well-being offers a holistic and nuanced approach to the complexities of human existence. It acknowledges the importance of pleasure and enjoyment while emphasizing the value of virtues and ethical living. Additionally, it embraces the existential challenge of confronting life's uncertainties and creating meaning in the face of the void. Ultimately, finding this balance is a profoundly personal and reflective journey, and individuals may draw on each philosophy in unique ways to navigate the intricate landscape of well-being.

Chapter 6: Happiness and Ethics

Imagine for a moment that happiness is not merely a fleeting emotion but a moral compass guiding our ethical choices and actions. In this innovative exploration of "Happiness and Ethics," we embark on a journey where well-being becomes the ethical lighthouse illuminating the path towards a more compassionate and virtuous world.

The Ethical Imperative of Happiness

At the heart of this innovative perspective lies the idea that happiness is not merely a personal pursuit but an ethical imperative. It posits that our actions and decisions should be evaluated based on their moral correctness and their potential to contribute to the overall well-being and happiness of individuals and communities.

The Happiness Ethics in Action

Imagine a world where ethical decision-making is intrinsically tied to its impact on happiness. In this world:

Business Ethics Redefined: Corporations prioritize the well-being of employees, customers, and society, recognizing that sustainable profit and happiness are not mutually exclusive. Ethical business practices revolve around creating products and services that genuinely enhance the quality of life.

Environmental Ethics Aligned with Well-being: Environmental ethics become synonymous with ensuring a flourishing planet for current and future generations. Actions are guided by the understanding that a healthy environment is foundational to human happiness, and decisions are made to protect and preserve it.

Global Ethical Responsibility: Nations and international organizations base their policies on the principle of global happiness and well-being. Cooperation, diplomacy, and aid efforts are driven by a commitment to reducing global disparities and enhancing the overall quality of life for all.

Ethical Healthcare and Education: In healthcare and education, the happiness ethic transforms these sectors. Healthcare prioritizes not only the treatment of illness but also preventive care and mental well-being. Education focuses on nurturing not just academic excellence but also emotional intelligence, resilience, and life satisfaction.

The Happiness Ethic and Virtue Ethics

This innovative perspective also finds resonance with virtue ethics, a philosophical approach that emphasizes the development of moral virtues as the foundation of ethical living. In the context of the happiness ethic:

Virtues as Pathways to Happiness: Virtuous living becomes synonymous with pursuing happiness. Virtues like compassion, empathy, and altruism are not just moral principles but also recognized as pathways to personal and collective well-being.

Ethical Role Models: Ethical role models are individuals who embody both moral virtues and happiness. They inspire others through their ethical actions and radiating a sense of contentment and joy that stems from their virtuous choices.

The Ethical Challenge of Subjective Well-being

One of the most innovative aspects of the happiness ethic is its recognition of the subjective nature of well-being. It acknowledges that what brings happiness varies among individuals and cultures. This recognition poses a unique ethical challenge: respecting and promoting diverse sources of well-being while maintaining a common ethical framework.

In this scenario:

1. **Cultural Diversity as an Ethical Asset:** Cultural diversity becomes an asset rather than a barrier to ethical consensus. Ethical frameworks adapt to accommodate different cultural understandings of happiness, recognizing that the pursuit of well-being can manifest in various ways.

2. **Respect for Individual Choices:** Ethical judgments become less prescriptive and more respectful of individual choices. As long as these choices do not infringe upon the well-being and rights of others, diverse paths to happiness are valued and protected.

The Ethical Fulfillment of Human Potential

Ultimately, the innovative perspective of the happiness ethic presents an ethical framework that seeks to fulfill human potential. It challenges us to not only consider what is ethically right but also what contributes to the highest levels of well-being for individuals and societies.

In this paradigm:

1. **Ethical Excellence:** Ethical excellence is not solely defined by adherence to rules and principles but by the positive impact on well-being. Ethical actions are those that elevate happiness and contribute to the full realization of human potential.

2. **Ethical Progress:** Ethical progress is measured not only by a reduction in unethical behavior but also by an increase in overall well-being. Societies and individuals strive not just for moral rectitude but for continuous improvement in happiness and quality of life.

In conclusion, this innovative perspective on "Happiness and Ethics" challenges us to rethink the relationship between ethics and well-being. It envisions a world where ethical choices are intrinsically linked to promoting happiness and where diverse paths to well-being are respected and valued. Happiness becomes the ethical lighthouse guiding us toward a more compassionate, virtuous, and fulfilling existence.

Moral Dilemmas in the Quest for Happiness: Navigating Ethical Challenges

The pursuit of happiness, while a universal aspiration, is not without its ethical complexities and moral dilemmas. As individuals seek to enhance their well-being, they often encounter situations where their pursuit of happiness conflicts with ethical principles, social norms, or the well-being of others. This exploration delves into some of the moral dilemmas that can arise in the quest for happiness.

1. The Ethics of Self-Interest vs. Altruism

One common moral dilemma revolves around the tension between self-interest and altruism. Individuals often grapple with the question of whether to prioritize their own happiness and well-being or act in ways that benefit others. This dilemma becomes particularly pronounced when pursuing personal happiness involves actions that may be perceived as selfish or inconsiderate of others' needs.

2. The Moral Implications of Pursuing Personal Ambitions

Pursuing personal ambitions and success can raise ethical questions about the means employed to achieve one's goals. Ambition can drive individuals to make choices that may compromise their ethical principles, such as engaging in cutthroat competition, exploiting resources, or neglecting social and environmental responsibilities.

3. Balancing Individual and Collective Well-being

The pursuit of happiness often involves choices that impact not only the individual but also the broader community or society. This dilemma highlights the ethical challenge of balancing personal well-being with the well-being of others. For example, should one prioritize their own financial success if it contributes to income inequality or environmental degradation?

4. Ethical Considerations in Relationships

Moral dilemmas frequently emerge in the context of relationships. Individuals may face choices between pursuing a romantic relationship that brings them happiness and adhering to ethical principles, such as honesty, fidelity, and respect for others' feelings. Navigating these dilemmas requires careful consideration of one's values and commitments.

5. The Influence of Consumerism and Materialism

Consumerism and materialism can lead to ethical quandaries in the quest for happiness. The relentless pursuit of material possessions and a lavish lifestyle can conflict with ethical values related to sustainability, responsible consumption, and social justice. Decisions about what to buy and how much to consume often carry ethical implications.

6. The Conundrum of Short-Term Pleasures vs. Long-Term Fulfillment

The pursuit of happiness can lead individuals to choose short-term pleasures over long-term fulfillment. This dilemma arises when individuals prioritize immediate gratification through behaviors such as excessive drinking, overindulgence in unhealthy foods, or impulsivity. These choices may undermine long-term well-being and pose ethical questions about self-control and responsibility.

7. Ethical Dimensions of Happiness Enhancement

Advancements in science and technology have opened up new possibilities for enhancing happiness through pharmaceuticals, bioengineering, or cognitive interventions. These innovations raise ethical concerns about the potential for altering human experiences of happiness in ways that may not align with natural or traditional concepts of well-being.

8. Cultural and Relativistic Ethical Dilemmas

Cultural variations in ethical values can introduce dilemmas in the pursuit of happiness, especially in multicultural contexts. What is considered ethically acceptable in one culture may clash with the values of another. Navigating these differences while respecting diverse perspectives can be a complex challenge.

Resolving Moral Dilemmas in the Pursuit of Happiness

Resolving moral dilemmas in the quest for happiness requires a nuanced and reflective approach:

> **Self-Reflection:** Engage in self-reflection to identify your core values and ethical principles. Clarify what matters most to you in the pursuit of happiness and align your actions accordingly.

> **Balancing Interests:** Strive to find a balance between self-interest and altruism. Recognize that your well-being is interconnected with the well-being of others, and ethical choices often involve considering the broader impact of your actions.

Long-Term Perspective: Consider the long-term consequences of your choices. Short-term pleasures may bring immediate happiness, but they may conflict with your long-term goals and values. Evaluate whether the pursuit of short-term happiness is worth compromising your long-term well-being.

Ethical Guidelines: Develop a set of ethical guidelines or principles that can guide your decision-making in morally complex situations. These guidelines can serve as a moral compass when facing dilemmas.

Seeking Ethical Guidance: In challenging ethical situations, seek guidance from trusted friends, mentors, or ethical professionals who can offer different perspectives and insights.

Cultural Sensitivity: When navigating cultural and relativistic ethical dilemmas, practice cultural sensitivity and open-mindedness. Be willing to learn from different cultural viewpoints and adapt your behavior when appropriate.

Ethical Growth: Recognize that ethical decision-making is a lifelong journey. Your understanding of ethics and your ability to navigate moral dilemmas may evolve over time.

The quest for happiness is a complex and deeply personal journey that often intersects with moral dilemmas. Navigating these ethical challenges requires a thoughtful and conscientious approach that considers both emotional well-being and the well-being of others and the broader ethical implications of one's choices.

The Ethics of Happiness: Balancing Personal Well-being and Moral Responsibility

Pursuing happiness is a fundamental human aspiration, but it is not a solitary journey. It is interwoven with ethical considerations that compel individuals to navigate a complex terrain where their personal well-being intersects with moral responsibilities toward others and society at large. This exploration delves into two key dimensions of the ethics of happiness: the individual pursuit of happiness and the broader ethical implications of one's happiness.

1. Individual Pursuit of Happiness: Balancing Self-Interest and Ethical Principles

The pursuit of personal happiness is deeply ingrained in human nature. It involves seeking fulfillment, contentment, and satisfaction in various aspects of life, such as relationships, career, and personal growth. However, this individual quest for happiness is not devoid of ethical considerations.

Balancing Self-Interest and Ethical Principles: At its core, the ethics of personal happiness revolves around finding a harmonious balance between self-interest and ethical principles. Here are some ethical dilemmas often encountered in this pursuit:

> **Honesty and Authenticity:** Ethical dilemmas can arise when individuals must decide whether to be completely honest and authentic in their relationships, even if it may lead to discomfort or conflict. Striking a balance between personal happiness and the feelings of others becomes a key consideration.

> **Respect for Autonomy:** Respecting the autonomy and choices of others, even when it may not align with one's personal interests, is a fundamental ethical principle. Decisions related to personal relationships and career pursuits often involve respecting the autonomy of others.

> **Resource Allocation:** The pursuit of personal happiness often involves choices about how resources are allocated. Individuals may face ethical dilemmas when deciding how to distribute limited resources, such as time, money, or attention, among competing interests.

> **Impact on Others:** Ethical considerations extend to assessing the impact of one's pursuit of happiness on the well-being of others. For example, personal ambitions may require sacrifices that affect family members or colleagues.

Balancing self-interest and ethical principles in the individual pursuit of happiness requires careful consideration of the consequences of one's choices on others and the alignment of personal values with moral values.

2. Broader Ethical Implications of Happiness: Beyond Individual Well-being

Happiness is not confined to the individual; it has ripple effects that extend to society and the world. Ethical considerations expand beyond one's personal pursuit of happiness to encompass the broader implications of happiness on a societal and global scale.

Responsibility to Society and the Common Good: The ethics of happiness includes a responsibility to consider the well-being of society and the common good. Several ethical dimensions arise in this context:

> **Social Responsibility:** Ethical dilemmas emerge when individuals and institutions must balance their pursuit of happiness with social responsibility. Businesses, for example, face ethical decisions related to fair labor practices, environmental sustainability, and community engagement.

> **Inequality and Justice:** The distribution of happiness and well-being within a society raises ethical questions about inequality and justice. The ethics of happiness compels individuals and societies to address disparities and advocate for policies that promote greater social equity.

> **Environmental Ethics:** The impact of human activities on the environment is a critical ethical concern tied to happiness. Moral choices about resource consumption, conservation, and sustainability have far-reaching consequences for the well-being of future generations.

> **Global Interconnectedness:** In an interconnected world, the ethics of happiness extends beyond national borders. Ethical dilemmas include questions about global economic justice, humanitarian aid, and the responsibility of affluent nations to address global challenges.

Conclusion: Balancing Individual Well-being and Ethical Responsibility

The ethics of happiness challenge individuals to navigate the intricate interplay between their personal well-being and moral responsibilities toward others and society. It requires a thoughtful consideration of ethical principles such as honesty, respect, justice, and social responsibility in the pursuit of happiness.

Balancing self-interest and ethical principles is an ongoing journey that calls for introspection, empathy, and a commitment to aligning personal values with ethical values. Moreover, recognizing the broader ethical implications of happiness underscores the importance of fostering individual well-being in ways that promote the greater good, social justice, and the sustainable well-being of our global community. Ultimately, the ethics of happiness invites individuals to find joy in their own lives and contributions to a more just and compassionate world.

Altruism and the Greater Good: Nurturing Compassion in a Complex World

Altruism, often defined as selfless concern for the well-being of others, is a moral compass that guides individuals toward actions that benefit the greater good. In an increasingly complex and interconnected world, the principles of altruism have never been more crucial. This exploration delves into the concept of altruism, its significance in promoting the greater good, and how individuals and societies can nurture and harness this powerful force for positive change.

Understanding Altruism: A Compassionate Drive

At its core, altruism represents the innate human capacity for compassion, empathy, and selflessness. It is the willingness to act for the benefit of others without expecting personal gain or reward. Altruistic acts can manifest in various forms, from simple acts of kindness to more significant contributions to the welfare of others or society.

The Greater Good: A Collective Well-being

The greater good encompasses the well-being and welfare of a collective, whether it be a community, society, or humanity as a whole. It acknowledges that individual interests are interconnected with the interests of the larger community and that actions taken for the benefit of others can ultimately enhance the well-being of all.

The Significance of Altruism for the Greater Good

Altruism plays a pivotal role in promoting the greater good in several key ways:

Social Cohesion and Harmony: Acts of altruism foster a sense of connection and unity within communities. When individuals look out for one another and support each other's well-being, it strengthens social bonds and promotes harmony.

Addressing Inequality: Altruistic actions can help mitigate social and economic inequality by redistributing resources and opportunities to those in need. Altruism acknowledges the moral imperative to bridge gaps in well-being and promote equity.

Crisis Response: In times of crisis, such as natural disasters or pandemics, altruism often shines brightly. Individuals and organizations mobilize to provide aid, support, and resources to those affected, showcasing the power of collective action for the greater good.

Community Resilience: Altruistic communities tend to be more resilient in the face of challenges. Communities can adapt and recover more effectively when individuals are willing to support one another during difficult times.

Moral Progress: Altruism contributes to moral progress by challenging and reshaping societal values. As people recognize the importance of empathy and compassion, societies become more attuned to the needs and rights of others, promoting justice and ethical development.

Nurturing Altruism: Strategies for Individuals and Societies

Altruism is a virtue that can be cultivated and nurtured at both individual and societal levels. Here are strategies to foster and harness altruism for the greater good:

1. Education and Awareness: Promote education that emphasizes empathy, compassion, and the importance of altruism. Encourage discussions about ethical behavior and its role in improving society.

2. Role Models and Inspirational Stories: Highlight individuals and organizations that embody altruism and have made a positive impact on the greater good. Inspirational stories can motivate others to follow suit.

3. Volunteerism and Community Engagement: Create opportunities for individuals to engage in volunteer work and community service. These experiences can cultivate a sense of empathy and social responsibility.

4. Encouraging Acts of Kindness: Emphasize the importance of small acts of kindness in daily life. Encouraging and acknowledging these acts can create a culture of generosity.

5. Fostering Inclusivity: Promote inclusive and diverse communities where individuals from different backgrounds and perspectives come together to work for the greater good. Inclusivity fosters a sense of belonging and shared responsibility.

6. Ethical Leadership: Leaders in various domains, including politics, business, and civil society, can set an example by prioritizing the greater good over self-interest. Ethical leadership inspires others to do the same.

7. Supportive Policies and Institutions: Governments and institutions can implement policies and initiatives that support altruistic behavior. This may include tax incentives for charitable donations or programs that facilitate community involvement.

8. Collective Action: Encourage collective action to address pressing societal issues. Altruism is often most potent when individuals come together to tackle challenges that no one person can solve alone.

Altruism as a Path to a Better World

Altruism is powerful for promoting the greater good, fostering compassion, and creating a more just and harmonious world. It challenges individuals and societies to recognize their interconnectedness and prioritize the well-being of all. Nurturing altruism, both individually and collectively, is a moral imperative and a pathway to a brighter and more compassionate future for humanity.

Chapter 7: The Science of Happiness

Happiness, a cherished and elusive state of well-being, has long been a subject of human fascination and inquiry. However, in recent decades, the field of psychology has delved into the science of happiness, unraveling its mysteries and providing evidence-based insights into how individuals can lead happier lives. This exploration delves into the fascinating realm of the science of happiness, shedding light on its key principles, research findings, and practical applications.

1. Defining Happiness: A Multifaceted Concept

The science of happiness begins with the challenge of defining happiness itself. Researchers have recognized that happiness is a multifaceted concept encompassing various dimensions, including:

Life Satisfaction: An overall assessment of one's life as a whole, considering various domains such as work, relationships, and health.

Positive Emotions: Experiencing moments of joy, contentment, gratitude, and other positive emotions.

Engagement: Experiencing a flow state, where individuals are fully immersed in a task and lose track of time.

Meaning and Purpose: Finding significance and fulfilment in life through a sense of purpose or contribution to others.

Positive Relationships: The quality of social connections and the presence of supportive and meaningful relationships.

2. The Pursuit of Happiness: What the Research Reveals

Over the past few decades, research in positive psychology—the study of well-being and human flourishing—has uncovered key insights into the pursuit of happiness:

Genetic and Environmental Influences: Happiness is influenced by a combination of genetic and environmental factors. While genetics play a role in one's baseline level of happiness, environmental factors, such as relationships, experiences, and activities, also significantly impact well-being.

Adaptation and Set-Point Theory: The concept of hedonic adaptation suggests that people tend to return to a relatively stable level of happiness (set-point) even after significant life events, whether positive or negative. This phenomenon challenges the idea that external circumstances alone can lead to lasting happiness.

The Importance of Positive Experiences: Positive experiences, such as savoring enjoyable moments, engaging in hobbies, and cultivating meaningful relationships, have a significant impact on well-being. Accumulating positive experiences contributes to long-term happiness.

The Role of Gratitude and Mindfulness: Practices like gratitude journaling and mindfulness meditation have been shown to enhance happiness. Gratitude encourages individuals to focus on positive aspects of life, while mindfulness fosters present-moment awareness and reduces stress.

Social Connections: Strong social connections are a powerful predictor of happiness. Meaningful relationships, support networks, and social engagement contribute to an individual's sense of well-being.

Purpose and Meaning: Finding a sense of purpose and meaning in life is associated with higher levels of happiness. Engaging in activities that align with one's values and contribute to the greater good can enhance overall well-being.

3. Practical Applications: Cultivating Happiness

The science of happiness offers practical strategies for individuals to cultivate well-being in their lives:

Positive Psychology Interventions: Positive psychology interventions, such as gratitude exercises, acts of kindness, and focusing on strengths, have been shown to increase happiness and life satisfaction.

Mindfulness and Meditation: Mindfulness-based practices, such as meditation and mindful breathing, can reduce stress, enhance emotional regulation, and increase happiness.

Pursuit of Flow: Engaging in activities that induce a state of flow, where individuals are fully absorbed in a task, can lead to a sense of accomplishment and happiness.

Strengthening Relationships: Nurturing and investing in meaningful relationships with family, friends, and the community can significantly contribute to happiness.

Cultivating Purpose: Exploring personal values, passions, and ways to contribute to society can help individuals find greater purpose and meaning in their lives.

The Ongoing Quest for Happiness

The science of happiness continues to evolve as researchers explore new dimensions of well-being and delve into the intricate interplay of factors that contribute to happiness. It reminds us that while genetics may set a baseline for our happiness, there are actionable steps individuals can take to enhance their well-being. Ultimately, pursuing happiness is a deeply personal journey guided by scientific insights, personal reflection, and intentional choices aimed at leading a more fulfilling and joyful life.

Positive Psychology: The Science of Well-being

Positive psychology is a pioneering field within psychology that focuses on understanding and promoting human well-being and flourishing. Unlike traditional psychology, which often concentrated on addressing mental illnesses and disorders, positive psychology seeks to explore the factors that contribute to a fulfilling and meaningful life. This exploration delves into positive psychology's principles, key components, and practical applications.

1. The Birth of Positive Psychology

Positive psychology emerged as a distinct field in the late 20th century, with Dr. Martin Seligman often credited as one of its founders. Seligman's presidential address to the American Psychological Association in 1998 marked a significant turning point. He called for a shift from the traditional focus on "disease" (i.e., mental illness) to the study of "strengths and virtues" and the promotion of well-being.

2. Core Principles of Positive Psychology

Positive psychology is grounded in several core principles:

Focus on Strengths: Positive psychology emphasizes identifying and harnessing individual and collective strengths rather than dwelling on weaknesses or pathology.

Scientific Rigor: Positive psychology applies rigorous scientific methods to investigate and validate its theories and interventions.

Holistic Well-being: It recognizes that well-being encompasses various dimensions, including emotional, social, physical, and psychological well-being.

Cultivation of Flourishing: The ultimate goal is to foster human flourishing, which goes beyond happiness to include aspects such as meaning, engagement, and purpose in life.

3. Key Components of Well-being

Positive psychology identifies several key components that contribute to human well-being:

Positive Emotions: Experiencing positive emotions like joy, gratitude, and love contributes to overall well-being.

Engagement: Being fully absorbed and engaged in activities, often referred to as "flow," enhances well-being.

Relationships: High-quality relationships and social connections are vital for well-being.

Meaning and Purpose: Finding meaning and purpose in life gives individuals a sense of fulfillment and direction.

Accomplishment: Setting and achieving meaningful goals and accomplishments are significant contributors to well-being.

4. Practical Applications of Positive Psychology

Positive psychology offers numerous practical applications that individuals can incorporate into their lives to enhance well-being:

Gratitude Practices: Keeping a gratitude journal, where individuals regularly reflect on things they are thankful for, can boost positive emotions and well-being.

Mindfulness and Meditation: Mindfulness practices, such as meditation and mindful breathing, help individuals stay present, reduce stress, and improve emotional regulation.

Strengths-Based Approaches: Identifying and using personal strengths can increase confidence and overall well-being.

Positive Relationships: Nurturing and investing in positive relationships with family, friends, and peers enhances social well-being.

Goal Setting: Setting and working toward meaningful goals can provide a sense of purpose and accomplishment.

Acts of Kindness: Engaging in acts of kindness and helping others has been shown to increase happiness and life satisfaction.

5. The Role of Resilience

Resilience, the ability to bounce back from adversity and maintain well-being, is another significant aspect of positive psychology. Resilience can be cultivated through strategies like building a growth mindset, developing coping skills, and seeking social support during challenging times.

6. Positive Psychology in Education and Workplaces

Positive psychology has found practical applications in education and the workplace. Schools and organizations have implemented programs and interventions based on positive psychology principles to enhance the well-being and performance of students and employees.

The Pursuit of Flourishing

Positive psychology shines a light on the pursuit of human flourishing and offers valuable insights and practical tools for individuals to lead more fulfilling and meaningful lives. It reminds us that well-being is not merely the absence of problems but the presence of strengths, positive emotions, and a sense of purpose. By incorporating the principles and practices of positive psychology into their daily lives, individuals can take proactive steps toward a more flourishing existence.

Measuring Happiness: Understanding the Science of Subjective Well-being

Happiness, as a complex and subjective emotional state, has posed a significant challenge to researchers and policymakers who seek to measure and understand it. However, advances in psychology and social science have led to the development of various methods and metrics for assessing happiness and subjective well-being. This exploration delves into the science of measuring happiness, examining the key approaches, factors, and implications of this endeavor.

1. Subjective Well-being: The Multi-dimensional Nature of Happiness

Subjective well-being (SWB), often used interchangeably with happiness, encompasses a broad range of subjective experiences related to well-being. It consists of three primary components:

> **Life Satisfaction:** An individual's overall assessment of their life as a whole, which takes into account various life domains, such as work, relationships, and health.

> **Positive Affect:** The frequency and intensity of positive emotions and feelings experienced in daily life, including joy, contentment, and gratitude.

> **Negative Affect:** The frequency and intensity of negative emotions and feelings experienced, including stress, anxiety, and sadness.

Measuring happiness involves assessing these components individually and collectively to comprehensively understand an individual's well-being.

2. Quantitative Measures of Happiness

Several quantitative measures and scales have been developed to assess happiness and subjective well-being. These include:

Satisfaction with Life Scale (SWLS): A widely used scale that asks individuals to rate their agreement with statements about their life satisfaction.

Positive and Negative Affect Schedule (PANAS): A questionnaire that assesses the frequency and intensity of positive and negative emotions experienced over a specified time period.

Subjective Happiness Scale (SHS): A measure that assesses overall subjective happiness by asking individuals to rate themselves on a happiness scale and answer questions about their happiness.

Cantril's Self-Anchoring Striving Scale: Also known as the "Ladder of Life," this scale asks individuals to rate their current and ideal life satisfaction on a scale resembling a ladder, with higher rungs indicating greater satisfaction.

3. Qualitative and Open-ended Approaches

While quantitative measures provide numerical scores, qualitative and open-ended approaches offer rich insights into individuals' experiences of happiness. These methods involve interviews, surveys, or diaries where participants provide detailed narratives about their well-being, describing the factors that contribute to their happiness and life satisfaction.

4. Factors Influencing Happiness Assessment

Various factors can influence how individuals assess their happiness and well-being:

Cultural Differences: Cultural norms and values shape individuals' perceptions of happiness. Some cultures prioritize individual happiness, while others emphasize collective well-being and harmony.

Social Comparison: People often assess their happiness relative to others, leading to relative deprivation or satisfaction based on social comparisons.

Adaptation: Hedonic adaptation refers to the tendency for individuals to return to a stable level of happiness despite significant life changes, which can influence self-reported well-being.

Context and Framing: The way questions are framed in surveys or interviews can influence responses. For example, asking individuals about their "life satisfaction" may yield different responses than asking about their "happiness."

Coping Mechanisms: People may underreport negative emotions or overreport positive emotions as a coping mechanism or social desirability bias.

5. Policy and Practical Implications

Measuring happiness has practical implications for policy, governance, and well-being interventions:

Policy Design: Governments and organizations can use happiness metrics to inform policy decisions related to education, healthcare, urban planning, and social welfare.

Well-being Interventions: Measuring happiness can help assess the effectiveness of well-being interventions and programs to improve individuals' lives.

National Well-being Indices: Some countries, like Bhutan with its Gross National Happiness index, have developed comprehensive well-being indices to guide policy decisions.

Conclusion: A Holistic Understanding of Well-being

Measuring happiness is a multidimensional endeavor combining quantitative and qualitative approaches to comprehensively understand an individual's subjective well-being. While the science of measuring happiness has made significant strides, it is important to recognize the subjectivity and cultural nuances inherent in assessing well-being. Ultimately, understanding happiness is a valuable tool for improving individual lives and shaping policies and interventions that contribute to the well-being of societies as a whole.

The Pursuit of Lasting Happiness: Beyond Ephemeral Pleasures

The pursuit of happiness is a fundamental human aspiration, but achieving lasting happiness requires a deeper understanding of the factors that contribute to enduring well-being. In a world often characterized by fleeting pleasures and instant gratification, the quest for lasting happiness calls for a shift in perspective. This exploration delves into the concept of lasting happiness, the challenges it presents, and the strategies to cultivate enduring well-being.

1. The Ephemeral Nature of Pleasure

In contemporary society, pleasure often takes center stage in the pursuit of happiness. Instant gratification, material possessions, and sensory indulgences can provide momentary satisfaction, but they tend to be short-lived. The ephemeral nature of pleasure highlights the distinction between momentary happiness and lasting well-being.

2. The Components of Lasting Happiness

Lasting happiness transcends fleeting pleasures and encompasses deeper dimensions of well-being:

Fulfillment and Meaning: Experiencing a sense of purpose and meaning in life provides a foundation for lasting happiness. Engaging in activities aligned with one's values and making meaningful contributions to others fosters enduring fulfillment.

Positive Relationships: Strong, supportive, and meaningful relationships are essential for lasting well-being. Building and nurturing connections with others contribute to a sense of belonging and emotional stability.

Resilience and Coping: Developing resilience and effective coping mechanisms equips individuals to navigate life's challenges with grace and adaptability. Resilience enables people to bounce back from setbacks and maintain a positive outlook.

Self-acceptance and Growth: Embracing self-acceptance and a growth mindset allows individuals to appreciate themselves as they are while striving for personal development. The pursuit of self-improvement can be a source of lasting happiness.

Mindfulness and Presence: Practicing mindfulness and being fully present in the moment reduce anxiety about the future and regrets about the past. This heightened awareness enhances overall well-being.

3. The Paradox of Choice

The modern world offers an abundance of choices, but the paradox of choice suggests that excessive options can lead to decision paralysis and decreased satisfaction. People may constantly seek new experiences or possessions in search of happiness, only to find that it remains elusive.

4. Adaptation and the Hedonic Treadmill

Hedonic adaptation is the tendency for individuals to return to a relatively stable level of happiness after experiencing significant life changes, whether positive or negative. This phenomenon challenges the notion that external circumstances alone can lead to lasting happiness. Winning the lottery or facing adversity may temporarily affect happiness, but people tend to revert to their baseline level of well-being.

5. Cultivating Lasting Happiness

Cultivating lasting happiness involves intentional practices and a shift in mindset:

Gratitude: Regularly expressing gratitude for the positive aspects of life fosters lasting well-being by focusing on what one has rather than what is lacking.

Savoring: Learning to savor enjoyable moments and experiences amplifies their impact on happiness.

Altruism: Acts of kindness and altruism, which benefit others, often lead to increased lasting happiness.

Simplicity: Simplifying one's life by decluttering both physical possessions and commitments can reduce stress and enhance overall well-being.

Self-compassion: Treating oneself with the same kindness and understanding as one would offer to a friend promotes lasting self-acceptance and happiness.

6. The Role of Perspective

Perspective plays a crucial role in the pursuit of lasting happiness. Shifting from focusing on external circumstances and fleeting pleasures to appreciating inner qualities, meaningful relationships, and personal growth can lead to enduring well-being.

The Journey to Lasting Fulfillment

The pursuit of lasting happiness invites individuals to embark on a journey of self-discovery and personal growth. It acknowledges that happiness is not a destination but an ongoing process that involves nurturing meaningful connections, finding purpose, and cultivating a mindset that appreciates the richness of life in all its dimensions. While momentary pleasures may bring temporary joy, lasting happiness resides in human existence's deeper, enduring aspects.

Chapter 8: Practical Pursuits of Happiness

Practical Pursuits of Happiness: Strategies for a Fulfilling Life

Happiness is a universal aspiration, but it often eludes us in the hustle and bustle of daily life. However, by adopting practical strategies and making intentional choices, individuals can enhance their well-being and pursue happiness meaningfully. This exploration delves into worthwhile pursuits of happiness, offering actionable steps and insights for leading a more fulfilling life.

1. Cultivating Positive Relationships

Meaningful and positive relationships are a cornerstone of happiness. To cultivate such relationships:

> **Invest Time and Effort:** Allocate time to nurture relationships with family and friends. Genuine connections require effort and attention.

> **Express Gratitude:** Show appreciation for the people in your life. Expressing gratitude fosters stronger bonds and positive emotions.

> **Practice Active Listening:** Be fully present when interacting with others. Listening attentively and empathetically enhances the quality of your relationships.

> **Resolve Conflicts:** Constructively address conflicts and misunderstandings. Effective conflict resolution can strengthen relationships.

2. Pursuing Personal Growth

Continuous personal growth and self-improvement contribute to happiness. To pursue personal growth:

> **Set Goals:** Define clear and achievable goals for different aspects of your life, whether they relate to career, education, or personal development.

> **Embrace Learning:** Be open to new experiences and opportunities for learning. Expanding your knowledge and skills can boost confidence and satisfaction.

Challenge Comfort Zones: Step out of your comfort zone and embrace challenges. Growth often occurs when you confront unfamiliar situations.

Practice Resilience: Develop resilience by learning to bounce back from setbacks and adversity. Resilience helps you navigate life's ups and downs with greater ease.

3. Fostering Physical and Mental Well-being

Physical and mental well-being are essential for happiness. To prioritize well-being:

Exercise Regularly: Engage in physical activities that you enjoy. Exercise releases endorphins and promotes mental and emotional health.

Maintain a Balanced Diet: Eat a well-balanced diet that nourishes your body and mind. Proper nutrition can impact mood and energy levels.

Practice Mindfulness: Incorporate mindfulness and meditation into your daily routine. These practices can reduce stress and enhance emotional well-being.

Get Adequate Sleep: Prioritize sleep to ensure your body and mind are well-rested. Quality sleep is crucial for overall well-being.

4. Nurturing Gratitude and Positivity

Cultivating gratitude and a positive mindset can significantly contribute to happiness:

Keep a Gratitude Journal: Regularly write down things you're grateful for. This practice shifts your focus toward the positive aspects of life.

Challenge Negative Thoughts: Practice cognitive reframing to replace negative thoughts with more positive and constructive ones.

Surround Yourself with Positivity: Spend time with people who uplift and inspire you. Positive social interactions can boost your mood.

Engage in Acts of Kindness: Perform acts of kindness for others. Acts of kindness not only benefit others but also enhance your sense of purpose and well-being.

5. Finding Meaning and Purpose

Living a life imbued with meaning and purpose contributes to a deep sense of happiness:

Reflect on Values: Identify your core values and beliefs. Align your actions and decisions with these values to find a sense of purpose.

Volunteer and Contribute: Engage in volunteer work or activities that allow you to positively impact others and the community.

Pursue Passions: Dedicate time to hobbies and interests that ignite your passion. Pursuing what you love can bring joy and fulfilment.

Set Meaningful Goals: Set goals that resonate with your values and aspirations. Achieving these goals can provide a sense of purpose.

6. Balancing Work and Leisure

Balancing work responsibilities with leisure and relaxation is crucial for well-being:

Set Boundaries: Establish clear boundaries between work and personal life. Disconnecting from work when you're off-duty is vital.

Prioritize Self-care: Dedicate time to self-care activities, such as hobbies, reading, or spending time in nature. These moments of relaxation recharge your energy.

Take Breaks: Incorporate short breaks during your workday to refresh your mind and reduce stress.

Plan Vacations: Schedule periodic vacations or getaways to unwind and rejuvenate.

7. Practicing Mindful Living

Mindful living involves being fully present in the moment and savoring life's experiences:

> **Practice Mindfulness:** Engage in mindfulness meditation and mindful breathing to develop present-moment awareness.

> **Savor Moments:** Slow down and savor everyday experiences, such as enjoying a meal, appreciating nature, or spending time with loved ones.

> **Disconnect from Technology:** Limit screen time and digital distractions to be more present in your daily life.

Conclusion: The Art of Intentional Living

Happiness is not a destination but a journey shaped by intentional choices and practices. By nurturing positive relationships, pursuing personal growth, prioritizing well-being, fostering gratitude and positivity, finding meaning and purpose, balancing work and leisure, and practising mindful living, individuals can embark on a path of intentional living that leads to a more fulfilling and happy life.

Cultivating Happiness: Strategies and Exercises for a Joyful Life

Happiness is not merely a fleeting emotion but a skill that can be developed and nurtured through intentional practices. Cultivating happiness involves adopting strategies and engaging in exercises that promote well-being and positive emotions. This exploration delves into practical techniques and exercises for producing happiness and enhancing the overall quality of life.

1. Gratitude Practice

Gratitude is a powerful tool for fostering happiness. Regularly practising gratitude helps shift your focus toward the positive aspects of life:

> **Gratitude Journal:** Dedicate a few minutes daily to write down three things you are grateful for. This simple exercise helps you become more aware of the positive elements in your life.

Express Gratitude: Reach out to people who have positively impacted your life and express your appreciation. Writing thank-you notes or having heartfelt conversations can deepen your sense of gratitude.

Gratitude Walk: During a walk or hike, take time to appreciate the beauty of nature and the simple pleasures of the outdoors. Reflect on the things you are grateful for in that moment.

2. Mindfulness Meditation

Mindfulness meditation promotes awareness of the present moment and reduces stress and anxiety:

Mindful Breathing: Practice mindful breathing by focusing on your breath. When your mind wanders, gently bring your focus back to your breath.

Body Scan: Conduct a body scan meditation to become aware of physical sensations and any areas of tension or discomfort in your body. This practice promotes relaxation and self-awareness.

Loving-Kindness Meditation: Engage in loving-kindness meditation to cultivate compassion and goodwill toward yourself and others. Send out wishes for happiness and well-being to yourself, loved ones, acquaintances, and even those you may have conflicts with.

3. Acts of Kindness

Performing acts of kindness for others not only brings joy to them but also enhances your happiness:

Random Acts of Kindness: Engage in random acts of kindness, such as paying for someone's coffee, holding the door open for a stranger, or leaving positive notes in public spaces.

Volunteer Work: Dedicate time to volunteer for a cause or organization you are passionate about. Giving back to the community fosters a sense of purpose and fulfillment.

Kindness Challenge: Set a kindness challenge for yourself to perform several kind acts each week. Challenge friends or family members to join you on this journey.

4. Positive Visualization

Positive visualization exercises help you envision a happier and more fulfilling future:

Future Self Visualization: Imagine your future self living a content and fulfilled life. Picture the goals you have achieved, the positive relationships you have, and the activities that bring you joy.

Gratitude Visit: Write a letter to your future self expressing gratitude for the positive experiences and achievements you anticipate. Seal the letter and open it at a later date to reflect on your progress.

5. Strengths-Based Approaches

Identifying and leveraging your strengths can boost self-esteem and overall well-being:

Strengths Assessment: Take a strengths assessment, such as the VIA Character Strengths Survey, to identify your core strengths. Once identified, find opportunities to use these strengths in your daily life.

Strengths Journal: Keep a journal where you record instances when you used your strengths and how they contributed to positive outcomes or well-being.

6. Positive Affirmations

Positive affirmations help reframe negative thought patterns and promote self-confidence:

Daily Affirmations: Create a list of positive affirmations tailored to your goals and well-being. Repeat these affirmations daily, either in front of a mirror or in writing.

Affirmation Cards: Create affirmation cards with short, impactful statements that you can carry with you throughout the day. Whenever you need a boost, read your affirmation cards.

7. Physical Activity

Exercise has a profound impact on mood and happiness:

Regular Exercise: Engage in regular physical activity that you enjoy, whether it's walking, dancing, swimming, or participating in team sports.

Outdoor Activities: Spend time in nature through hiking, biking, or picnicking. Nature has a calming and rejuvenating effect on the mind.

Conclusion: The Ongoing Journey to Happiness

Cultivating happiness is an ongoing journey that involves practicing gratitude, mindfulness, kindness, self-awareness, and self-compassion. Incorporating these strategies and exercises into your daily life can enhance your well-being, build resilience, and foster a more joyful and fulfilling existence. Remember that happiness is not a destination but a way of life; your efforts to cultivate it will contribute to a more meaningful and contented life.

The Role of Relationships and Social Connections in Happiness

Human beings are inherently social creatures, and the quality of our relationships and social connections profoundly affects our overall happiness and well-being. This exploration delves into the significance of relationships and social connections in fostering happiness, their impact on mental and physical health, and strategies for nurturing and enhancing these crucial aspects of life.

1. The Significance of Social Connections

Emotional Support: Social connections provide emotional support during challenging times and offer a sense of belonging and security.

Reduced Stress: Positive social interactions and strong relationships have been linked to reduced stress levels, leading to better mental and physical health.

Enhanced Resilience: Supportive social networks help individuals cope with adversity and bounce back from setbacks, enhancing their resilience.

Happiness Multiplier: Sharing joyful moments and experiences with others magnifies the happiness experienced, making it more enduring.

2. Types of Social Connections

Family: Family relationships are often the earliest and most enduring bonds we form. The support and love of family members contribute significantly to overall well-being.

Friends: Friendships offer companionship, shared experiences, and a sense of belonging. Close friendships can be a source of emotional support and happiness.

Romantic Relationships: Intimate partnerships provide emotional intimacy, love, and companionship. Happy romantic relationships can lead to increased life satisfaction.

Community and Social Groups: Engaging in community activities, clubs, or social organizations fosters a sense of community and belonging.

3. The Impact of Social Connections on Health and Well-being

Mental Health: Strong social connections are associated with lower rates of depression and anxiety. On the other hand, loneliness is a risk factor for mental health issues.

Physical Health: Social isolation can adversely affect physical health, increasing the risk of conditions such as heart disease and hypertension. In contrast, social support can boost the immune system and promote overall well-being.

Longevity: Studies have shown that individuals with robust social networks tend to live longer, healthier lives.

4. Strategies for Nurturing Social Connections

Active Listening: Practice active listening when engaging with others. Paying genuine attention to what others say fosters deeper connections.

Quality Time: Prioritize quality time with loved ones. Put away distractions and focus on being present during interactions.

Open Communication: Encourage open and honest communication in your relationships. Share your thoughts, feelings, and concerns, and be receptive to others' perspectives.

Cultivate New Relationships: Seek out opportunities to meet new people and expand your social circle. Join clubs, attend social events, or engage in activities aligned with your interests.

Acts of Kindness: Perform acts of kindness for others, even small ones. Acts of kindness can strengthen existing relationships and create new ones.

Manage Conflict: Conflict is a natural part of relationships. Learn healthy conflict resolution skills to address disagreements constructively.

5. Building and Maintaining Close Relationships

Invest Time and Effort: Building and maintaining close relationships requires effort and time. Dedicate resources to nurturing the relationships that matter most to you.

Show Appreciation: Express your appreciation and gratitude for the people in your life. Simple acts of kindness and acknowledgement can strengthen bonds.

Shared Experiences: Create and share meaningful experiences with loved ones. These shared moments create lasting memories and strengthen connections.

Emotional Support: Be a source of emotional support for others, and don't hesitate to seek support when needed.

6. Overcoming Loneliness

Reach Out: If you're feeling lonely, contact friends, family, or support groups. Don't be afraid to initiate contact and express your feelings.

Volunteer: Engaging in volunteer work can provide opportunities for social connections while contributing to a sense of purpose.

Seek Professional Help: If loneliness persists and impacts your mental health, consider seeking support from a therapist or counselor.

Conclusion: The Heartbeat of Happiness

In the grand tapestry of human existence, relationships and social connections are the threads that weave happiness into our lives. Cultivating and nurturing these connections is essential for our well-being and a fundamental aspect of what it means to be human. By valuing and investing in our relationships, we can experience deeper, more enduring happiness and create a positive ripple effect that extends to those around us.

The Impact of Mindfulness and Gratitude on Well-being

Mindfulness and gratitude are two powerful practices that profoundly impact well-being, fostering happiness, reducing stress, and promoting mental and emotional health. This exploration delves into the significance of mindfulness and gratitude, their individual and collective effects, and practical ways to incorporate these practices into daily life.

1. The Power of Mindfulness

- **Mindful Awareness:** Mindfulness involves being fully present in the moment paying non-judgmental attention to thoughts, feelings, and sensations. It encourages a state of heightened awareness.

- **Stress Reduction:** Mindfulness practices like meditation and mindful breathing are effective tools for reducing stress and anxiety. By focusing on the present moment, individuals can manage the impact of stressors.

- **Emotional Regulation:** Mindfulness helps individuals become more attuned to their emotions and responses. It promotes emotional regulation by providing space to observe feelings without judgment.

- **Enhanced Well-being:** Regular mindfulness practice has increased life satisfaction, greater overall well-being, and improved mental health.

2. The Practice of Gratitude

Cultivating Gratitude: Gratitude involves recognizing and appreciating the positive aspects of life, whether big or small. It encourages a shift in focus from what is lacking to what is present.

Positive Emotions: Practicing gratitude fosters positive emotions, such as joy, contentment, and happiness. It counters negative thought patterns and promotes optimism.

Improved Relationships: Expressing gratitude to others strengthens relationships, deepens connections, and fosters a sense of belonging.

Resilience: Gratitude can enhance resilience by helping individuals cope with adversity and find meaning in challenging situations.

3. Mindfulness and Gratitude in Harmony

Complementary Practices: Mindfulness and gratitude are complementary practices. Mindfulness creates the space for individuals to notice and appreciate the positive aspects of life, enhancing the practice of gratitude.

Gratitude Journal with Mindfulness: One effective way to combine these practices is to keep a gratitude journal. Set aside time each day to mindfully reflect on the things you are grateful for and record them.

Mindful Gratitude Meditation: Engage in mindful gratitude meditation sessions. During these sessions, focus on gratitude for specific aspects of your life, such as relationships, health, or personal achievements.

Gratitude in Mindful Moments: Throughout the day, practice moment-to-moment mindfulness by paying attention to the beauty and positivity present in your surroundings and interactions.

4. Practical Ways to Incorporate Mindfulness and Gratitude

Morning Routine: Start your day with a few moments of mindfulness and gratitude. Reflect on your gratitude and set positive intentions for the day ahead.

Mindful Eating: Practice mindful eating by savoring each bite of your meals. Express gratitude for the nourishment your food provides.

Nature Walks: Spend time in nature and use this opportunity to practice mindfulness. Observe the sights, sounds, and sensations of the natural world with appreciation.

Technology Breaks: Take breaks from technology to disconnect and engage in mindfulness and gratitude practices. Put away screens and focus on the present moment.

Bedtime Reflection: Before sleep, reflect on the day and identify moments of gratitude. Express thanks for the positive experiences and relationships you encountered.

5. The Lasting Effects on Well-being

Both mindfulness and gratitude have lasting effects on well-being:

Resilience: These practices enhance resilience, enabling individuals to navigate life's challenges more easily.

Positive Outlook: They promote a positive outlook on life, fostering optimism and a sense of hope.

Improved Mental Health: Mindfulness and gratitude contribute to improved mental health by reducing symptoms of depression and anxiety.

Enhanced Relationships: The positive emotions generated by these practices strengthen relationships and deepen connections.

Conclusion: The Path to a Fulfilling Life

Mindfulness and gratitude are pathways to a fulfilling life marked by happiness, contentment, and emotional well-being. By incorporating these practices into daily life, individuals can develop a greater appreciation for the present moment, nurture positive emotions, reduce stress, and enhance their overall sense of well-being. These practices remind us that external circumstances do not solely determine happiness but is within our grasp through intentional cultivation of inner peace and gratitude

Chapter 9: The Pursuit of Happiness in a Changing World

In an ever-evolving world marked by rapid technological advancements, shifting societal norms, and global challenges, the pursuit of happiness takes on new dimensions and complexities. This exploration delves into the ways in which individuals can navigate the pursuit of happiness in a changing world, adapt to challenges, and embrace well-being in the face of uncertainty.

1. The Changing Landscape of Happiness

Technological Advancements: Technology has transformed the way we connect, work, and live. While it offers convenience, it also presents challenges related to screen addiction, information overload, and disconnection from authentic human experiences.

Social Dynamics: Changing societal norms and values impact how individuals form relationships, find purpose, and define happiness. Evolving family structures and gender roles are reshaping traditional concepts of happiness.

Global Challenges: The world faces complex issues like climate change, pandemics, economic disparities, and political instability. These challenges can generate anxiety and uncertainty, affecting well-being.

2. Adaptation and Resilience

Hedonic Adaptation: People naturally tend to adapt to changes in their circumstances, whether positive or negative. Pursuing happiness requires an awareness of this adaptation process and intentional efforts to maintain a positive outlook.

Resilience: Building resilience equips individuals to navigate life's uncertainties and challenges. Resilience involves developing coping skills, seeking support, and finding meaning in adversity.

3. Shifting Perspectives on Happiness

Beyond Materialism: Happiness is increasingly recognized as extending beyond material possessions in a changing world. Pursuing experiences, meaningful connections, and personal growth takes precedence over consumerism.

Eudaimonic Well-being: The pursuit of eudaimonia, or flourishing, emphasizes the importance of living a purpose-driven life. Finding meaning, engaging in self-improvement, and contributing to the greater good are central to this approach.

4. The Role of Mindfulness and Adaptability

Mindfulness: Mindfulness practices, such as meditation and mindful living, foster resilience and adaptability. They help individuals stay grounded in the present moment and cultivate a greater sense of inner peace.

Adaptability: In a changing world, adaptability is a valuable trait. Embracing change with an open mindset, seeking growth opportunities, and learning to let go of what no longer serves one's well-being are key aspects of adaptability.

5. Finding Purpose and Meaning

Seeking Purpose: Pursuing happiness often involves seeking a sense of purpose. Exploring one's passions, values, and aspirations can lead to discovering a purpose-driven life.

Contributing to Others: Happiness is often found in contributing to the well-being of others and the community. Acts of kindness and altruism provide a sense of fulfilment and connection.

6. Well-being in a Global Context

Cultural Variations: Different cultures have unique perspectives on happiness. Understanding and respecting cultural variations in pursuing happiness is essential in a globalized world.

Global Solidarity: Addressing global challenges, such as climate change and health crises, requires international cooperation and a sense of global solidarity. Working together to tackle these issues can contribute to a collective sense of purpose and well-being.

7. Navigating Uncertainty

Mindful Decision-Making: In uncertain times, making decisions mindfully and with intention can reduce anxiety. Weighing options, considering consequences, and seeking guidance when needed are valuable practices.

Self-Compassion: Practicing self-compassion during challenging periods is crucial. Being kind to oneself, acknowledging limitations, and seeking support are essential aspects of self-care.

Conclusion: Embracing the Journey of Well-being

Pursuing happiness in a changing world is an ongoing journey marked by adaptation, resilience, and a deep exploration of what truly matters. It requires a shift in perspective, embracing mindfulness, and a commitment to finding meaning and purpose in a dynamic and uncertain environment. By cultivating adaptability and fostering well-being on a personal and global scale, individuals can navigate the challenges of our changing world and find happiness amid transformation.

Technological Advances and the Digital Age: Navigating Opportunities and Challenges

The rapid evolution of technology and the emergence of the digital age have reshaped every facet of human life, from communication and work to education and entertainment. This exploration delves into the profound impact of technological advances in the digital age, the opportunities they present, and the challenges they pose to individuals and society as a whole.

1. The Digital Revolution

Connected World: The advent of the internet and smartphones has connected people like never before. Information flows freely, and communication is instant.

Digital Transformation: Industries have undergone significant digital transformation. The digital age has disrupted traditional norms, from e-commerce and telemedicine to remote work and online learning.

2. Opportunities in the Digital Age

Access to Information: The digital age grants unparalleled access to information, fostering learning and knowledge-sharing.

Remote Work and Flexibility: Technology enables remote work, offering flexibility and work-life balance to many professionals.

Economic Growth: Technological advancements drive economic growth by creating new industries and job opportunities.

Innovation: The digital age fuels innovation, from artificial intelligence and machine learning to sustainable technologies and space exploration.

3. Challenges and Concerns

Digital Divide: Disparities in internet access and digital literacy create a digital divide, limiting opportunities for marginalized communities.

Privacy Concerns: The collection and sharing of personal data raise privacy concerns. Data breaches and surveillance threaten individual privacy.

Mental Health: Excessive screen time and social media use can contribute to mental health issues, including anxiety and depression.

Cybersecurity: The digital age brings the risk of cyberattacks, hacking, and data breaches that can have far-reaching consequences.

4. Impact on Communication

Social Media: Social media platforms have revolutionized communication, offering connection and potential for misinformation and online harassment.

Global Reach: Digital communication transcends geographical boundaries, allowing people to connect with others worldwide.

Filter Bubbles: Algorithms personalize content, potentially trapping individuals in echo chambers of like-minded views.

5. Education and Learning

Online Learning: The digital age has transformed education with online courses and remote learning options.

Access to Education: Technology provides access to education for people in remote or underserved areas.

Challenges: Online learning also presents challenges, such as the digital divide and the need for self-motivation.

6. The Future of Work

Remote Work: Remote work is on the rise, offering flexibility but also blurring the lines between work and personal life.

Automation: Automation and AI may reshape the job market, leading to concerns about job displacement.

Upskilling: Lifelong learning and upskilling become essential in a rapidly changing job landscape.

7. Ethical Considerations

Ethical AI: Ethical concerns surround the development and use of artificial intelligence, including bias and fairness issues.

Digital Ethics: The digital age prompts discussions on digital ethics, data ownership, and responsible technology use.

Navigating the Digital Frontier

The digital age brings unprecedented opportunities and challenges. Navigating this dynamic landscape requires a blend of digital literacy, ethical awareness, adaptability, and critical thinking. Embracing the benefits of technology while addressing its drawbacks is essential to harness the full potential of the digital age and ensure it serves the betterment of individuals and society as a whole.

Environmental Challenges and Personal Happiness: The Interplay Between the Planet and Our Well-being

The connection between environmental challenges and personal happiness is a multifaceted and deeply intertwined one. Our environment, including the air we breathe, the water we drink, and the natural landscapes we inhabit, profoundly impacts our overall well-being and, by extension, our happiness. This exploration delves into the intricate relationship between environmental challenges and personal happiness, highlighting the ways in which our surroundings can affect our mental and emotional states.

1. Air Quality and Respiratory Health

Impact on Happiness: Poor air quality due to pollution can directly affect personal happiness by compromising respiratory health. Individuals in areas with high pollution levels may experience increased rates of respiratory diseases, such as asthma and bronchitis, which can lead to physical discomfort and emotional distress.

2. Access to Natural Spaces

Impact on Happiness: Proximity to natural spaces, such as parks, forests, and bodies of water, has been linked to increased happiness and well-being. Nature provides opportunities for relaxation, recreation, and a sense of wonder that can enhance personal satisfaction.

3. Biodiversity and Psychological Well-being

Impact on Happiness: The presence of diverse flora and fauna in natural environments can positively impact psychological well-being. Experiencing a rich variety of species can evoke feelings of awe and connectedness, contributing to overall happiness.

4. Water Quality and Health

Impact on Happiness: Access to clean and safe drinking water is a fundamental human need. Contaminated water sources can lead to waterborne diseases, which can severely impact health and happiness. Ensuring clean water can provide peace of mind and contribute to well-being.

5. Natural Beauty and Aesthetic Pleasure

Impact on Happiness: Scenic landscapes and natural beauty can inspire aesthetic pleasure, fostering joy and happiness. Appreciating nature's aesthetics is a source of emotional well-being for many individuals.

6. Environmental Stress and Mental Health

Impact on Happiness: Environmental stressors, such as natural disasters, climate-related events, or the loss of natural landscapes due to urbanization, can lead to mental health challenges, including anxiety and depression. Losing cherished natural spaces can evoke grief and sadness, impacting personal happiness.

7. Personal Actions for Well-being

Impact on Happiness: Engaging in eco-friendly behaviors and protecting the environment can contribute to personal happiness. Many individuals find fulfillment in reducing their carbon footprint, conserving resources, and contributing to environmental sustainability.

A Holistic Approach to Happiness

Environmental challenges and personal happiness are deeply interconnected, as the state of our environment can significantly influence our mental and emotional well-being. Recognizing this interplay underscores the importance of a holistic approach to happiness that considers not only personal choices and social factors but also the health and sustainability of the planet. By advocating for and nurturing a healthy environment, individuals can enhance their own happiness and contribute to the well-being of future generations. In this symbiotic relationship between environmental health and personal happiness, lies the potential for a more harmonious and fulfilling existence

Reimagining Happiness for Future Generations: Sustainable Well-being in a Changing World

The pursuit of happiness is an enduring aspiration that transcends time and generations. However, as we look to the future, it becomes increasingly essential to reimagine happiness in a changing world characterized by environmental, technological, and societal shifts. This exploration delves into reimagining happiness for future generations, emphasizing the need for sustainable well-being that prioritizes balance, resilience, and the flourishing of both individuals and the planet.

1. Rethinking Materialism

Shift from Consumerism: Reimagining happiness involves shifting away from a consumer-driven mindset that equates possessions with well-being. Future generations may find greater fulfillment in experiences, relationships, and personal growth rather than material accumulation.

Sustainable Consumption: Promoting sustainable consumption and conscious consumer choices can align personal happiness with environmental well-being, ensuring that future generations inherit a planet capable of supporting their needs.

2. Digital Well-being

Mindful Technology Use: As technology continues to evolve, future generations may emphasize mindful and intentional technology use. They may prioritize digital well-being by balancing screen time and offline experiences.

Digital Detox: Recognizing the importance of disconnecting from screens, future generations might adopt periodic digital detoxes to recharge, reconnect with nature, and foster in-person social connections.

3. Environmental Stewardship

Connection to Nature: Reimagining happiness involves nurturing a deep connection to nature. Future generations may prioritize environmental stewardship, recognizing that a thriving planet is essential for their own well-being.

Sustainable Lifestyles: Sustainability may become an integral part of daily life for future generations, influencing choices related to transportation, energy consumption, and resource management.

4. Holistic Health and Well-being

Emotional and Mental Health: Future generations may prioritize emotional and mental well-being as much as physical health. Strategies for coping with stress, building resilience, and fostering positive mental health could be integrated into education and daily life.

Preventive Health: The emphasis on well-being may lead to a focus on preventative health measures, reducing the burden of chronic diseases and enhancing overall life satisfaction.

5. Education for Sustainable Living

Holistic Education: Education systems may evolve to prioritize holistic learning, including emotional intelligence, environmental literacy, and ethical values. Future generations may be better equipped to make informed, sustainable choices.

Global Citizenship: Education could foster a sense of global citizenship, encouraging individuals to consider the well-being of the global community and future generations' decision-making.

6. Inclusive Societies

Social Equity: Future generations may strive for more equitable societies, recognizing that well-being is interconnected with social justice. Inclusivity and diversity may be celebrated as sources of strength and happiness.

Community Building: Building strong, supportive communities may become a central aspect of well-being, as individuals recognize the value of social connections in times of change and uncertainty.

7. Ethical Leadership and Governance

Leadership Values: Ethical leadership that prioritizes the everyday good and long-term sustainability may be increasingly valued by future generations. Ethical decision-making at all levels of governance can contribute to societal happiness.

Interconnected Policies: Policies addressing environmental protection, social welfare, and economic stability may be integrated to create a comprehensive framework for well-being.

The vision of Sustainable Happiness

Reimagining happiness for future generations involves envisioning a world where individual well-being harmonizes with the planet's and society's well-being. It is a vision of sustainable happiness that transcends fleeting pleasures and material gains, prioritizing balance, resilience, and the flourishing of individuals and the Earth. By embracing this vision and taking proactive steps to enact change, we can create a future where happiness is synonymous with well-being, and future generations inherit a world worth living in.

Chapter 10: The Philosophy of Happiness: Reflections and Prospects

The philosophy of happiness is a timeless and ever-evolving field of inquiry that seeks to unravel the nature of human well-being and the pursuit of a fulfilling life. In this reflection, we explore the current state of the philosophy of happiness, its historical evolution, and the prospects it holds for shaping a more meaningful and harmonious future.

1. Historical Foundations

The quest to understand happiness has deep historical roots, spanning cultures, traditions, and philosophical schools of thought:

> **Aristotle's Eudaimonia:** Aristotle's concept of eudaimonia, or flourishing, remains influential. He posited that true happiness is achieved through virtuous living and realising one's potential.

> **Hedonism and Utilitarianism:** Philosophers like Epicurus and Bentham explored hedonistic and practical approaches to happiness, emphasizing pleasure and the minimization of pain as central to well-being.

> **Eastern Philosophies:** Eastern philosophies, such as Buddhism and Taoism, offer unique perspectives on happiness, often centred on mindfulness, detachment from desire, and inner peace.

2. Contemporary Philosophical Debates

In the contemporary era, the philosophy of happiness has given rise to nuanced debates and diverse perspectives:

> **Subjective vs. Objective Well-being:** Scholars grapple with the distinction between subjective well-being (individual feelings of happiness) and objective well-being (conditions that promote happiness). The balance between the two is a matter of ongoing discussion.

Happiness and Virtue: Virtue ethics, which focuses on character development and moral excellence, continues to influence discussions on the relationship between ethics and happiness.

Cultural and Cross-Cultural Perspectives: Contemporary philosophy of happiness considers the influence of culture on well-being, acknowledging that definitions and sources of happiness can vary widely across cultures.

3. Prospects and Emerging Themes

The philosophy of happiness is poised to address pressing issues and shape the future in several ways:

Environmental Ethics: Given the urgency of ecological challenges, philosophers are exploring how a sustainable, harmonious relationship with nature can be integral to human happiness.

Technological Ethics: The digital age introduces ethical questions about the impact of technology on well-being, privacy, and the nature of authentic human experiences.

Global Ethics: In an interconnected world, discussions on global ethics and the well-being of all humans, regardless of nationality or background, are gaining prominence.

Positive Psychology: Collaborations between philosophy and positive psychology are expanding our understanding of well-being, emphasizing the importance of character strengths, resilience, and life satisfaction.

4. Practical Applications

The philosophy of happiness is not confined to academia; it has practical implications for individuals, communities, and societies:

Well-being Policies: Some governments are incorporating well-being indicators into policy-making, recognizing that measures like Gross Domestic Product (GDP) do not capture the full spectrum of societal well-being.

Moral and Ethical Decision-Making: Philosophical happiness insights inform ethical frameworks guiding personal and collective decision-making.

Personal Reflection: Individuals can draw on philosophical ideas to reflect on their own sources of happiness, values, and life goals.

5. The Ongoing Quest

The philosophy of happiness remains an ever-evolving field, reflecting humanity's timeless quest for a meaningful and fulfilling existence. As we navigate the complexities of a changing world, the pursuit of happiness, enriched by diverse philosophical perspectives, offers a compass to guide us toward a future where well-being is a personal aspiration and a shared societal goal. In this ongoing quest, philosophy continues to illuminate the path to a more thoughtful, ethical, and harmonious way of living.

The Ever-Evolving Philosophy of Happiness: From Ancient Wisdom to Modern Exploration

The philosophy of happiness is a dynamic field of inquiry that has evolved over millennia, adapting to the changing contexts of human existence. From ancient wisdom to modern exploration, this reflection traces the evolution of this philosophy and its enduring relevance in today's world.

1. Ancient Foundations

Aristotle's Eudaimonia: In ancient Greece, Aristotle introduced the concept of eudaimonia, often translated as "flourishing" or "well-being." He argued that true happiness is achieved through cultivating virtue and realising one's potential.

Hedonism and Epicureanism: Philosophers like Epicurus and his school of thought, Epicureanism, emphasized pursuing pleasure and avoiding pain as central to human happiness.

Eastern Philosophies: Eastern philosophies, including Buddhism and Confucianism, offered distinct perspectives on happiness. Buddhism, for instance, teaches that liberation from suffering is attainable through the Eightfold Path and the cultivation of mindfulness.

2. Enlightenment Era and Utilitarianism

The Enlightenment: The Enlightenment era ushered in new philosophical perspectives on happiness. Thinkers like Jeremy Bentham introduced utilitarianism, which posits that the greatest happiness for the greatest number should guide moral and ethical decisions.

3. Contemporary Exploration

Positive Psychology: In recent decades, positive psychology has emerged as a field dedicated to the scientific study of human well-being and happiness. Researchers like Martin Seligman focus on character strengths, resilience, and life satisfaction.

Subjective Well-being: Contemporary discussions often revolve around the concept of subjective well-being, which encompasses individuals' own assessments of their happiness and life satisfaction.

Cross-Cultural Perspectives: Contemporary philosophy of happiness acknowledges the diversity of cultural perspectives on well-being, emphasizing the need for cross-cultural understanding and respect.

4. Relevance in the Modern World

The philosophy of happiness remains relevant in the modern world for several reasons:

Environmental Ethics: Given the pressing environmental challenges, philosophers explore how sustainable relationships with nature contribute to human well-being.

Technological Ethics: As technology transforms human existence, ethical questions about its impact on well-being, privacy, and human connection continue to arise.

Global Ethics: In an interconnected world, discussions on global ethics and the well-being of all individuals, regardless of nationality, gain prominence.

Personal Guidance: Individuals draw on philosophical insights to reflect on their own sources of happiness, values, and life goals.

5. An Ever-Evolving Quest

The philosophy of happiness is not static but a living and evolving field. It reflects humanity's enduring quest for meaning and fulfilment in the face of changing circumstances. As we navigate the complexities of a rapidly changing world, this philosophy provides a timeless compass that guides us toward a more thoughtful, ethical, and harmonious way of living. It reminds us that pursuing happiness is not a destination but a journey enriched by the wisdom of the past and the exploration of the present, offering insights into how we can lead more fulfilling lives.

The Quest Continues: Future Directions in Happiness Studies

Happiness studies, a field that explores the nature of well-being and the pursuit of happiness, continuously evolves to adapt to the changing landscape of human existence. As we peer into the future, several exciting directions and prospects emerge, guiding the ongoing quest for a deeper understanding of what it means to lead a fulfilling life.

1. Interdisciplinary Collaboration

Confluence of Disciplines: The future of happiness studies will see even greater collaboration between fields such as philosophy, psychology, sociology, economics, neuroscience, and environmental science. This interdisciplinary approach will offer richer insights into the multifaceted nature of happiness.

Holistic Understanding: Embracing diverse perspectives will lead to a more holistic understanding of well-being, recognizing that happiness encompasses not only individual emotions but also social, cultural, and ecological dimensions.

2. Technological Advancements

Positive Technology: Integrating positive psychology with technology will result in the development of positive technology applications, such as well-being apps and virtual reality experiences, designed to enhance personal happiness and mental health.

Big Data and Well-being: Advanced data analytics will allow researchers to analyze vast datasets related to happiness, providing valuable insights into the factors that influence well-being at both individual and societal levels.

3. Environmental Well-being

Ecological Happiness: Environmental ethics and sustainability will become increasingly integrated into happiness studies. Researchers will explore how our relationship with the environment affects our well-being and the well-being of future generations.

Nature-Based Interventions: The therapeutic benefits of nature will be harnessed through practices like ecotherapy and forest bathing, contributing to both mental and environmental well-being.

4. Cultural and Global Perspectives

Cultural Pluralism: Future research will acknowledge the diversity of cultural perspectives on happiness. This pluralistic approach will emphasize the importance of respecting and understanding various definitions and sources of well-being.

Global Well-being: Ethical considerations will drive discussions on global well-being, urging societies to consider the well-being of all humans, regardless of nationality or background, in policy-making and decision-making processes.

5. Ethical and Moral Foundations

Ethical Reflection: Philosophical exploration of the ethical foundations of happiness will remain crucial. Delving into questions of virtue, morality, and the common good will provide valuable guidance for individuals and societies.

Moral Psychology: Researchers will delve deeper into the moral and ethical dimensions of happiness, investigating how moral values and actions influence personal well-being and the well-being of communities.

6. Personal Transformation

Mindfulness and Resilience: Practices that cultivate mindfulness and resilience will continue to gain prominence in well-being studies. These practices help individuals navigate life's challenges and enhance their overall sense of happiness.

Character Development: The study of character strengths and virtues and the promotion of character education will play a central role in personal transformation and well-being enhancement.

7. Policy and Societal Implications

Well-being Policies: Governments and organizations will increasingly adopt well-being metrics and consider happiness and quality of life when designing policies and programs. The aim is to prioritize the overall well-being of citizens over economic growth alone.

Work-Life Balance: The importance of work-life balance and flexible work arrangements will be emphasized as societal values shift towards holistic well-being.

8. Education for Well-being

Holistic Education: Educational institutions will incorporate holistic well-being into their curricula, teaching emotional intelligence, resilience, and character development alongside academic subjects.

Global Citizenship Education: Education will foster a sense of global citizenship, encouraging students to consider their roles in creating a more just and compassionate world.

A Bright Horizon

Happiness studies will evolve and expand into exciting and uncharted territories as the quest for happiness continues. The field will deepen our understanding of individual well-being and inspire collective efforts to create a world where happiness is not just a personal aspiration but a shared societal goal. The future of happiness studies holds the promise of a brighter, more fulfilling future, where human flourishing is at the heart of our endeavors.

Thoughts on the Pursuit of a Meaningful Life

Pursuing a meaningful life is a profound and enduring quest that transcends cultural, temporal, and individual boundaries. As we reflect on this timeless pursuit, several key insights emerge, offering guidance and inspiration for those seeking to infuse their lives with purpose, fulfillment, and significance.

1. The Quest for Meaning is Intrinsic

Meaning is not an external commodity to be acquired or achieved but an intrinsic aspect of human existence. Each person carries within themselves the capacity to discover and create meaning in their life's journey.

2. It's a Dynamic and Personal Journey

The search for meaning is a dynamic, ever-evolving, deeply personal journey. What brings meaning to one person's life may differ significantly from another's. This diversity of paths is a testament to the richness of human experience.

3. Meaning Can Be Found in Many Dimensions

Meaning is multifaceted and can manifest in various dimensions of life:

Pursuit of Passion: Passion and enthusiasm for one's interests and endeavors can infuse life with purpose and meaning.

Connections and Relationships: Deep, meaningful connections with others, built on empathy, love, and shared experiences, contribute significantly to a meaningful life.

Contributing to Others: Acts of kindness, altruism, and service to others often provide profound sources of personal meaning.

Personal Growth: The journey of self-discovery and personal growth can be intrinsically meaningful.

Philosophical Reflection: Delving into philosophical and ethical questions can offer insight and meaning, guiding one's actions and decisions.

4. Challenges are Integral

Challenges, setbacks, and even suffering are integral to the human experience. They can serve as catalysts for growth, resilience, and deepening one's sense of meaning. Embracing adversity as part of the journey is a testament to the resilience of the human spirit.

5. Mindfulness and Presence Matter

Cultivating mindfulness and being fully present in each moment can uncover layers of meaning in life's ordinary and extraordinary aspects. By savoring the present, individuals often discover a profound sense of purpose in the here and now.

6. The Search for Meaning is Ongoing

Pursuing a meaningful life is not a destination but an ongoing process. It requires continuous introspection, self-discovery, and adaptation as one's values, aspirations, and circumstances evolve.

7. Sharing Meaning with Others

Sharing one's sense of meaning with others can amplify its significance. Building connections and communities centered around shared values and purposes can enhance the collective pursuit of meaning.

8. Contribution to a Greater Good

Contributing to the greater good through personal actions, community involvement, or global initiatives can elevate one's sense of meaning. Working towards a world that reflects one's values and principles can be deeply fulfilling.

9. The Legacy of a Meaningful Life

A life imbued with meaning leaves a lasting legacy. It shapes the lives of others, influences the course of history, and leaves behind a resonance that extends far beyond one's time on Earth.

10. Embracing the Journey

Ultimately, the pursuit of a meaningful life is a journey worth embarking on. It may not always be easy, and the path may be winding and uncertain, but the discoveries, connections, and personal growth that accompany this pursuit make it a remarkable and enriching expedition.

In the end, the quest for meaning is a testament to the resilience, creativity, and profound capacity for growth that define the human spirit. It invites individuals to explore the depths of their existence, forging a path towards a life that is not merely lived but truly and authentically experienced with purpose and meaning.

About the Author

Evangeline Brooks is a fresh voice in the world of philosophical exploration. "The Art of Being Happy: A Philosophical Exploration" marks her debut work, showcasing her deep curiosity about the nature of happiness and her talent for making complex ideas accessible to all readers. Drawing inspiration from her background in philosophy and her passion for personal well-being, Evangeline's book offers a thought-provoking and insightful journey into the art of finding joy and meaning in life. Her genuine enthusiasm for the subject shines through in her engaging exploration of happiness and its profound philosophical dimensions.